MANAGEMENT
and the
Christian worker

MANAGEMENT
and the
Christian worker

By OLAN HENDRIX

CHRISTIAN LITERATURE CRUSADE
Fort Washington, Pennsylvania 19034

CHRISTIAN LITERATURE CRUSADE
Fort Washington, Pennsylvania 19034

CANADA
1440 Mackay Street, Montreal, Quebec

First published in 1970
by
EVANGELICAL LITERATURE SERVICE,
Madras, India

Revised edition published in 1972
by
LIVING BOOKS FOR ALL, Asian Division
P.O. Box 513, Manila, Philippines

SBN 87508-232-7

This American edition published in 1973 by special
arrangement with LIVING BOOKS FOR ALL, Asian
Division, for sale in the U.S.A. and Canada only.

CONTENTS

FOREWORD

For a number of years it has been my privilege to be associated with Mr. Olan Hendrix in different inter-mission programs, including IFMA Mission Administration Seminars. During this time Mr. Hendrix has demonstrated a real gift for communicating management principles to Christian workers. His studies are based upon the Bible and incorporate solid concepts gained from a thorough study of management literature. His lectures have stimulated pastors, missionaries and executives of numerous organizations to seriously consider the relationship between good management and the effective outreach of their ministry.

National church leaders and missionaries of a number of third world countries have expressed to me their deep appreciation for the assistance they received by participating in a seminar led by Mr. Hendrix. It is significant that these lectures were first put into book form in India at the request of local Christian workers. Shortly thereafter, while in Africa I was delighted to see that copies had already been ordered by the African Christian leaders. Now this revised edition will enable many more servants of the Lord to profit from this helpful material, here in North America and elsewhere.

I am happy to commend this introductory book for study and implementation to staff and lay workers in all types of church organizations. Every office should have this important management book.

Edwin L. Frizen, Jr., Executive Secretary
Interdenominational Foreign Missions Association
Ridgefield Park, New Jersey, U.S.A.

THE AUTHOR

Rev. Olan Hendrix was born in Benton, Arkansas in the year 1928. He has attended Tennessee Temple College, King's College, the University of Deleware and Tennessee Temple Baptist Theological Seminary. He served for two years with the U.S. Navy in the Orient during World War II.

Rev. Hendrix has served as Pastor of First Baptist Church, Elkton, Pennsylvania (1950-1953) and Hilltown Baptist Church, Hilltown Pennsylvania (1953-1959). He was Home Secretary of the Far Eastern Gospel Crusade (1959-1969) and was Pastor of the Bethel Baptist Church, Kalamazoo, Michigan (1969-1970). At the present time he is General Director of the American Sunday School Union, with headquarters in Philadelphia, Pennsylvania.

The author makes his home in Merion, Pennsylvania, near Philadelphia, with his wife and five children. He is in constant demand as a conference speaker, lecturer in Management Seminars for Christian workers in many countries, serves as management consultant for various Christian organizations, is Chairman of the Cooperation and Comity Committee of the Interdenominational Foreign Missions Association, and is a member of the Boards of the West Indies Mission and Philadelphia College of Bible.

INTRODUCTION

We are faced with a subject which for some of us is going to be new. Let me suggest the kinds of questions that are going to come to your mind. You are going to wonder first, "Is this spiritual or is this a carnal deviation from trusting the Holy Spirit?" You are going to wonder, "Is it Biblical? How can this apply to Christian work?" People often say, "This is all very good, but how can you apply it when you don't sign the man's paycheck every week, and don't have the right to fire him?" There are answers to these and other questions. However, do not let questions prevent you from receiving the instruction which alone can answer them. We can easily close our minds so that there is no possibility of learning. The subject is new, something of an innovation, and yet there are answers here for spiritual men.

First, a definition — what do we mean by management or leadership? The word 'management' may sound too authoritative or too worldly for you. Then choose your own word. It does not matter what words we use so long as we understand from one another what is meant by these words. Aristotle said, "All of our difficulty comes from our failure to define terms." This is true — whether we talk about the boss, the director, the supervisor, the leader, or the manager. This is quite beside the point. The person referred to is in charge of a group of human beings for the accomplishment of a mutually-agreed purpose. I will use the words management and leadership quite interchangeably.

Let me suggest several definitions. It appears to me that management in Christian circles is basically the stewardship of the talents of the men entrusted to our care. Regardless of where you are, you have people with whom you work. If you are in position of leadership at all, you may not have much to say about who these people are and you certainly have very little to say about what their capacities or gifts are. However, you bear a solemn responsibility to exercise the stewardship of the talents of those men whom God has entrusted to your care. Basically, it is not for you to choose — and we often would choose men with different capacities if we had the option — but we do have the responsibility of exercising careful stewardship of the talents of these men. In missions and church activities I have observed serious abuse at this very point. We often disregard a man's God-given capacity and gifts, sometimes to the satisfaction of our own prejudices, and force them into moulds or activities for which God the Holy Spirit has not equipped them. Our job as leaders is to exercise Spirit-directed stewardship over these talents. It is for us to increase to the utmost the performance of the men that God has brought into our own ranks, with regard to our own personal gifts or capacities.

Lawence A. Appley says, "**Management is getting things done through other people.**" How is this important for us in Christian work? I am tremendously impressed with this. If ever anything is to be done in this broken world of ours, it is going to be done as we, who are called and sent of God, develop the awareness of the necessity for getting things done through other people. **Getting things done through other people.** We must involve other people. I discovered soon after God saved me that I was never going to be able to fulfil the burden of my own life personally — I was going to have to involve myself with other people. Not just anything, but **prescribed things** done through others. It is so much easier, it is the coward's way out, to conclude that we are going to do what we can do ourselves and we are not going to worry about what anybody else does. I had a friend, pastor of a little church in Maine, U.S.A. He had been there for years and years preaching to a handful of people. I said to him one day, "What in the world are you doing?" He was doing every menial task in the church, many of which could have been turned over to high school students or to men in the church. His answer appeared pious and commendable. Actually, it was very tragic. He said, "I do everything myself. I run off my own bulletins. I wash the windows in the church. I put out the hymn books. I do everything myself. This way I know it is done properly." We must develop the mentality, the attitude, that makes us involve other people. Jesus Christ did this. Our ministry is not only directed to people but it also involves accomplishing our purpose through people. It is not only **my** ministry to this broken world, but it is me reproducing myself in people with whom I am closely associated so that they minister to this broken world too. So, by way of definition I would insist that **management is getting things done through other people.**

Basically, management is a set of skills that an ordinary person can acquire and develop. Management is a kind of work which you can learn to perform. One important word as we study management is WORK — a kind of work which we perform. And the whole emphasis is going to be upon this idea.

You see someone effectively managing or leading a group of people and you are apt to think, "That looks easy. Let me get at it. I can do that." And we jump in and try. Recently friends were visiting us in Detroit. I took their teen-age boys water-skiing along with my own boys. One boy, about 15 years old, said, "I'd like to ski too." I asked, "Do you know how, Bobby?" "Oh, yes, yes." So I agreed. He got out and I noticed that when I pulled the rope up taut, his skis were very uncertain, but I thought, "Well, he's a little shaky." Finally he got them straightened out and when I raced the engine, skis and legs and arms went all over the place! I pulled back around, harnessed him up and tried again — and again legs and arms and skis went in all directions. After about the fourth time I pulled back around by him and said, "Bobby, do you know how to ski?" "Yes, I know how to ski." I thought better of the question and said, "Bobby, have you ever ski'd?" And he replied, "No, but it looks easy." And I thought, it is that way with leadership. You stand a few feet back and watch a fellow effectively leading a group and you think, "Oh, that's easy." You just smile, say a few words, write letters and lead meetings. You give orders and receive reports and it is great — until you try it and then it is not so easy! It requires skills that very few of us possess naturally.

Now, occasionally a man comes along who can 'manage by the seat of his pants!' Let me explain that. Back in World War I, I am told, the pilots in the era preceding the fantastic navigational aids that we enjoy today used to tell whether they were flying right side up in the clouds or wrong side up by where the pressure was. If the pressure was on the seat of their pants, they were right side up! If the pressure was on their seat belts, they were wrong side up! Some people manage by the seat of their pants, that is, if it feels right, if it feels comfortable. Or, if intuitively or instinctively you think that is the thing to do or that is not the thing to do, then all is well and good. The problem is that few people are equipped to manage by the seat of their pants. This is why we need to learn these skills. You must identify these skills, and I may not help you very much to acquire these skills but I will certainly show you how to go about acquiring them. We are looking at management as a work to be performed, as skills to be acquired.

On one occasion before I left home, my six-year-old boy was trying to learn to ride a bicycle. Oh, what mistakes! You got him going, and he'd bang into the side of the house or into a tree or something else! Then I received a letter which stated that John has now made it — he can ride now without running into something. One day he said, "Daddy, it looks so easy." "It does look easy, John, but there are some things you have to do. You have to keep going; you have to keep the wheels going in the right direction. You need to steer it and feel the balance. When you feel it going one way you have to pull back the other way." He said, "Yes, but it looks so easy." There are a lot of things that look easy but they require learning certain skills. There are times when you develop these skills to where they become second nature. They become instinctive. You are not conscious that you are practising these skills — like driving a car. After a while it becomes second nature. You just do it — but somewhere you learned it and you have to abide by these rules.

TOOLS FOR SPIRITUAL MEN

Management is a skill, but it is also a set of tools for spiritual men. It can be used by people who are not spiritual at all for ulterior and worldly purposes. By the same token, spiritual men can take these tools and use them for the glory of God and for the furtherance of the work of Jesus Christ. The whole point is not whether these tools are spiritual or not — **the whole point is whether WE are spiritual or not.** Let us not argue with the skills or the tools but with the condition of our own hearts. The issue is, "Am I a spiritual man?" If so, these tools can be worthwhile implements in the hands of a spiritual man.

Now if you want to be carnal in your service for Jesus Christ, you do not have to use management skills in order to do so. You can be carnal in your work for Christ without any management skills. In a slovenly way, in an unbusinesslike way, in a haphazard way, you can be carnal. The using of these skills does not mean that you are carnal, nor does the absence of them mean that you are spiritual. Be careful about that assumption. Let us not hide under that. The fact that I do not develop and study these skills does not mean that I am spiritual.

Here is a quotation that I want to sink so deeply into your consciousness that you will never, never forget it. The value of a sermon is not how much you say, it is determined by that one thing your audience cannot forget. An old pastor in the state of Ohio made this observation — **"There are some things God will bless as a supplement that He will curse as a substitute."** I am not talking at all about substitution.

Instinctively, invariably, someone will say,

"Isn't this a substitute for the fulness of the Holy Spirit?" No!

"Isn't this a bypassing for the responsibilities of the exposition of the Word?" No!

"Isn't this a shortcut to try to circumvent the necessity for believers being drawn together in spiritual unity?" No!

It is not a substitute for anything. It is a **supplement.** It is a set of tools for spiritual men.

This is why it is so important that we understand one another, that we get started off right on this spiritual foundation. The issue is not the spirituality of management. The issue is the spirituality of the man. We spend our lives arguing about the spirituality of things. Things are not spiritual; men are, or are not.

Is the subject of organizing scriptural? — Is it Biblical? Can we honestly study this subject giving the Word of God the pre-eminence in guiding our thinking? I think we can. I believe that every basic, honourable principle in industrial management has its root and foundation in the Word of God.

Take, for example, the life of Joseph. Is there in all of history a more magnificent example of leadership than Joseph? Preparing for that monumental harvest, then the horrible years of famine, delegating the work, planning the whole operation, distributing the materials, the food-stuffs, satisfying the complaints and handling the grievances — all are there. The people he had to work with were no better than the people you and I work with. As a matter of fact, he might have had worse people than some of us have. A magnificent example of organization in Scripture! And did God just drop it down into his brain so that he did it instinctively without ever thinking? I do not think so. God seldom works that way with men. Generally, He will guide us to the subjects we need to study and learn.

Or take Nehemiah and his exploits. If you read the book of Nehemiah carefully, and seek to find the management principles in it, you will discover that it contains every major management principle.

Is there organization in Scripture? I think so. Dr. Robert Coleman in his book, THE MAS-TER PLAN OF EVANGELISM, goes through the life of the Lord Jesus in His relationship with the apostles and he shows His selection of them, then

His association with them, impartation, demonstration, delegation, supervision and reproduction. There were intense organizational activities in the life of the Lord Jesus and in His relations with His disciples.

I attended a management seminar taught by Louis A. Allen, probably the foremost management researcher in America today. When he came to the subject of delegation he said, "I've got one example of delegation for you—Moses." Here you have a classic example of delegation in the Word of God. Delegation did not solve all the problems, but it solved the major ones. It created some others, but any time you solve one problem you create other problems. The last question you always ask yourself when you implement a decision to solve a problem is, "What is going to go wrong when I implement this decision?" Anytime you solve one problem, you are probably going to create some others.

I want to show you something about the administration in the Church of the Lord Jesus Christ. Romans 12:8 says, "Or he that exhorteth, let him wait on exhortation; he that giveth, let him do it with simplicity; he that ruleth, with diligence." (A.V.)   The Cambridge Bible says "ruleth" means to "preside whether in church or in any point of the work." It goes on to say that "with diligence" means "in haste, with earnestness, with laborious and minute attention to duty." It is always interesting to me that we are so apologetic in our attitude toward our positions of responsibility. Why is this? I think there are some reasons for it psychologically. We need to put our shoulders back and hold our heads high and say, "I am the director, I am the chairman, I am whatever I am by the appointment of a sovereign God." We underestimate ourselves and cause others to value us below God's estimation of us. This is not to grasp after position. We are not to count this position as something to be grasped after. "Let this mind dwell in you which was also in Christ Jesus." We are to have the mind of Christ. But we are not talking about status. We are talking about work, about a divine assignment of work and a performance of skills. It would mean a lot to the security of our people if they looked to us and found us confident — "This is the work God has given me to do." It is Biblical, is it not? God gives these capacities to men and then He gives men to the Church for specific purposes (Eph. 4:11-12). What happens if we belittle it? This is one of the reasons we are in trouble in evangelicalism, because we have underestimated our leadership ability.

The next thing to consider is, "Why is this subject neglected?" The first reason is ignorance. We simply do not know. It never occurred to most of us to study leadership as a set of skills that might be acquired like you study apologetics, hermeneutics, etc. My orientation was preaching. That is all I ever wanted to do. I got out of bed

one morning and found myself a manager!   I was
not alone — other people in our mission were in
the same boat.   What do you do?   You "fly by
the seat of your pants!"   You do what you feel
is right or what you think is right or what you
hope is right.   Of course you pray and ask for
guidance, but you are basically ignorant.

Then, one day one of our board members
came along and said, "Olan, you are in trouble."
I knew that.   My only consolation was that I was
not alone.   Our mission had outgrown a very
satisfactory form of government.   Normally an
organization comes into being with a certain form
of government.   However, it will outgrow the
demand for that style of leadership and demand
a new style of leadership as it goes through
various structures and stages.   This is why most
organizations emerge, flourish, and then flounder!
They cannot make the transition into a new era.
We were in real trouble — demoralization had
set in.   Our best men were threatening to leave.
We were following a hyper-democratic form of
government, and I have no argument against that.
(The Baptist form of government, you know, is
heavenly and that is the only place where it is
going to work!)   I am not teaching any form of
government in this course.   I am teaching management principles that will work in any form
of government.   If you go away from here thinking you have got to change some form or constitution, you have missed the whole point of the
course.   Four years ago when I got involved with

this subject my first temptation was to try to change our constitution. I thank the Lord that a wise fellow came along and said, "You do not need to do that." Here is what would happen— we would have a meeting and elect a chairman. Now a chairman is a manager. Someone will say, "Oh, no, no, we are just one big happy family and he merely leads the meetings." Then you are a traitor. Somebody has got to be in charge. We would get together and elect a leader. Do you know who we would elect? The best preacher we had! "Oh, listen to him pray. Isn't that beautiful? Put his name down. Listen to him preach! Oh, he had meetings and a hundred people came forward. Oh, let us make him our leader." So you take his Bible and pulpit away, give him a swivel chair behind a desk and say, "Administer! Manage!" We inflict irreparable damage on people because we elect them to ad-ministrative posts to which they are not equipped naturally. We refuse to recognize that they need specific preparation for that kind of work. Then when they do not perform up to our expectations we scold them! I can show you this same pattern in many missions. Why? Because we have not recognized that it is a work, that skills are demanded; and we have equated this whole busi-ness with "Oh, he is a good preacher and we will make him our chairman."

So this board member came along and said, "If I pay your way to a seminar, will you go?" Well, at that point I would have jumped off a bridge if I thought it would have helped. We were in trouble. So I attended a seminar, and as I sat there and listened to this man talk about the application of management principles to co-operative human efforts I said, "That will work! That is our problem! There is where we have missed it!" The ignorance began to be dispelled. It was not easy; I had a lot of ingrained prejudices and I had to overcome them, and I am still having to overcome them.

Another reason why we neglect this subject is that our traditional concept of leadership is the SNL concept — the Strong Natural Leader. Now when God saved me and called me to preach, all I wanted to do was preach. I wanted to learn how to preach, how to be a missionary. Later, I wanted to learn how to be a pastor when I knew I could not go to China. I thought to myself, "I am going to learn how to preach and how to get things done." So I went away to college. And lo and behold, I did not know a SNL from anything else, but here at this college there was a SNL in charge, and the college was in close proximity to a big church. I would go in and sit down and say, "I am going to watch how he does it!" This SNL — a SNL of the first order — would get up and let his congregation have it straight from the shoulder! So when I would get the opportunity to preach out in a small country church, I would get up and let them have it straight from the shoulder, and they would toss me out by my ear! I would then pull myself together and go back the next Sunday and say, "Do it again. I missed something." Again, he would let them have it straight from the shoulder. I have seen that man get up and call on four or five deacons to pray when he knew they were not there, just to embarrass them in front of 2,000 people. All right, that is the way you do it — you embarrass people. I would go out and embarrass people. Ugh! Out I would go! Well, I did not know that this man was a SNL. But you see, we try to emulate a Strong Natural Leader.

Occasionally a strong natural leader comes along and salvages an existing organization. Generally, however, the strong natural leader starts his own organization. Now a student came along one time when I was in college, looked at my library such as it was, and he said, "Look, all you have is Greek, Hebrew, apologetics and philosophy. Where are your biographies?" I replied, "Why do I need them? I am going to preach." He said, "You need to read biographies." So I went out and bought some biographies and autobiographies. It is a strange thing. Do you know that most biographies are written about SNL's? That did not help me — it hindered me. I found myself spending some nights in prayer, asking God to make me a SNL. I did not know that term, but I had Wesley, Taylor, Studd, Whitfield, Edwards, Spurgeon and others in my mind. I wanted to be like them. Listen, that is bondage. You have to accept yourself as you are. It was like getting out of jail when I awakened one day to discover that God wants me just as I am. I am not talking in a moral sense but in the sense of personality and with capacity. God has made me as I am. God has equipped me as I am equipped. He has divided these gifts to every man according to His wisdom. Well, this was wonderful! But in our own mission how slow we have been to recognize this.

The strong natural leader is often successful — **highly** successful — **but usually only over a short period of time.** Unless he dies or is displaced, the SNL often becomes his organization's worst enemy. I discovered that I am not a SNL. There is an alternative, and **the alternative** is **the professional leader** or the **scientific leader** or the **developed leader.** We mean, the man who does not have the dominating personality to draw people to himself automatically, to cause them to do what he wants them to do: the person who is an ordinary human being like you or me who develops the skills and engages in this kind of work.

Now, I am not concerned with the SNL. The SNL seldom attends a "leadership conference." He does not need to. Ordinary persons like you and me who are in positions of leadership can develop some of these skills. This is the whole point that we are dealing with: **how to develop these skills.** So we want to discover how to implement these skills in the situation in which we find ourselves.

The SNL will almost inevitably become the leader of the group, sometimes to his own detriment, often to the detriment of the whole organization. If there is one in our midst, he will gravitate to the top. This is inevitable. But the point is what do we do with that man if we do not build into him some of these skills which he is lacking? A SNL usually excels in one area only. In our ranks, the SNL is usually a good preacher. When he does not adequately manage, even though he is a good preacher, the group will turn against him.

This lecture is foundational. I do not think there can be any agreement or understanding concerning the subsequent lectures without a clear understanding of this introduction.

CHAPTER I

THE FUNCTIONS AND ACTIVITIES OF MANAGEMENT

I. **Function:**   **Management Planning**

   ACTIVITIES: Estimating
                   Establishing objectives
                   Developing policies
                   Programming
                   Establishing procedures
                   Scheduling
                   Budgeting

II. **Function:**   **Management Organizing**

   ACTIVITIES: Developing organization
                       structure
                   Delegating
                   Establishing relationships

III. **Function:**   **Management Leading**

   ACTIVITIES: Decision making
                       (brainstorming)
                   Communicating
                   Motivating
                   Selecting people
                   Developing people

IV. **Function:**   **Management Controlling**

ACTIVITIES: Establishing performance standards
Performance measuring
Performance evaluating
Performance correcting

Taken from **The Management Profession,** by Louis A. Allen, page 68 (McGraw-Hill).

Everything that is involved in any managerial situation can be plugged in under one of these **four main headings** or one of the **nineteen subpoints.** Everything! This is true in a highly complex managerial situation, e.g. General Motors. Even two people working together to accomplish a mutually-agreed objective apply the same principles. These are the management principles or issues for the successful accomplishment of that managerial situation. Simple or complex, these are the issues at stake.

The outline is broken down into four parts. Louis Allen calls them functions: Planning, Organizing, Leading and Controlling. My purpose is to go through this list, defining these terms very briefly with the hope that we can unify our terminology to mean a specific thing. We will look into these subjects individually and see how they relate to Christian work. This grouping is not in any order. You do not plan before you organize or before you lead or before you develop.

These are just put down this way because you have to put them down some way. We are trying to get all of this neatly filed so that you can immediately know where to go for the kind of information you need. As a matter of fact, I have set up my file just like this — planning, leading, organizing and controlling. It makes a better acrostic—PLOC. I have a file for each of these main points and each of the subpoints. Everytime I find something on the subject of leadership that I want to retain I file it in one of these places. I find that everything written on the subject of leadership can fit easily into one of these slots.

What do we mean by these terms? I will give very brief definitions.

MANAGEMENT PLANNING

PLANNING is the work we do to predetermine a course of action. Or, planning is throwing a net over tomorrow to cause to come to pass the thing we want to come to pass. The alternative to planning is chance and just letting things evolve as they will.

ESTIMATING is the work we do to estimate what tomorrow is going to be like. Many of us say we do not know. This is all the more reason why we need to engage in the work of estimating.

Because of the rapidity with which changes are taking place today, we need to appraise as accurately as possible what tomorrow is going to be like.

ESTABLISHING OBJECTIVES is the work we do to determine goals or targets. I venture to say that many of you reading this do not know why, definitively, you are on the mission field. Do not get mad at me — do not get cross — just wait. The hardest work I have ever done in all these years in the gospel ministry is the work of determining cooperatively the objectives of the North American Division of Far Eastern Gospel Crusade (FEGC). I have yet to meet a pastor who can answer me in a few words "Pastor, what is the objective of your church? Why is your church in existence?" Some of us do not know. We think we do. I thought I did. You would be surprised how much confusion there is in respect to goals and objectives in Christian work. This, more than anything else, contributes to our ineffectiveness. You can be filled with the Holy Spirit and anointed of the Spirit for ministry and not be joined together with definitive goals within your group.

POLICIES are standing answers to recurrent questions. Normally, in missions we confuse policies and objectives. A young person will come up to me in a Bible Conference and ask, "What are your mission policies?" What he often means is, "What are your mission objectives?"

PROGRAMMING is establishing the priority and sequence of activities for the accomplishment of our goals or objectives.

PROCEDURES is standardizing the methods of work, and probably we are more lax in missions than in any other phase of human co-operative effort. A young man is thrown into a piece of work and told to do it, but he is not allowed to benefit from what has been corporately learned by other people who have gone before into similar types of work. Everybody should benefit from what others have learned about doing a particular type of work. I have actually seen this sort of thing happen. A young missionary out of language study is assigned to a town and told, "Start a church here." Start a church? What do I do now? Here is a Japanese town utterly secularized and materialistic and preoccupied, with no need of God or the Gospel, and this young man is supposed to start a church. No one says, "Here is all we have learned from what we have been doing so far. We still do not know everything, but here is what little we do know. We want you to benefit from it so that you can get the job done most economically in time and effort."

SCHEDULING is putting a time factor on your programme, inserting the calendar into the programme with dates, hours and minutes. Let us understand the mind of the Lord when He expects a certain thing done and then let us co-operate with the Holy Spirit.

BUDGETING concerns more than just money! A new convert was asked by the treasurer of our mission, "Art, what are your impressions of missionaries?" He had several. This man is an advertising executive and he said, "The missionaries that I have known put proper evaluation on money, but no evaluation on time." I would tend to agree. We are talking about men, time, care and equipment, as well as money. It is the application of all of your resources.

MANAGEMENT ORGANIZING

ORGANIZING is the work in which we group and relate work to be performed. Whenever you think of organizing, you probably think of something like charts, blocks, lines — these blocks representing people and titles: Director, Superintendent, Chairman, Supervisor, etc. Organizing is tying together activities under an umbrella and in one human being for the accomplishment of the goal. Organizing is necessary to prevent fragmentation and the dissipation of activities and energies. Unless we organize, we have people doing what is noble and right and good and commendable but not bringing into strict discipline all of the activities of their lives and resources for the accomplishment of the purpose. Organizing does not have to be complicated. It does not make any difference how you do it, whether you have a chart or not. It means each human being knows what work he is responsible for and he knows it definitively. There are three aspects to organizing:

First, DEVELOPING ORGANIZATION STRUCTURE. In developing the structure, we group and relate the work and we relate people one to another — relating people one to another in their performance and in their authority, not just responsibility but in their authority as well.

Second, DELEGATION. There is more misunderstanding about delegation perhaps than any other single aspect of management. Delegating is the assigning of: (1) Responsibility, or if you prefer, work.   (2) Authority, that is, showing a person how much authority he has, what kind of decisions he can make, how far he can go. He must not only know what he is to do but how much money he can spend, how many decisions he can make, how many people he can handle or control, and how much time he can devote to it. But that is only a part of delegation. You do not stop there. You have not delegated — you have abdicated — and this is where most people get into trouble in delegation. (3) Accountability, establishing lines of accountability. The person who delegates not only says, "Will you do this piece of work?" and "Here is the authority you need in order to perform that job." He also says, "I will check back with you Friday afternoon at two o'clock to see how you are making out."

Do you know why we do not establish lines of accountability and delegation? Many of us are afraid of people; we do not like people. This involves us "eyeball to eyeball" with people, in direct personal encounter with people. Also this takes time, and most of us are too busy preaching to manage. If we will blend harmoniously these three ingredients in delegation, we can improve the performance of our organization tremendously. But remember, you must have all three aspects: work, authority, and accountability.

Third, ESTABLISHING RELATIONSHIPS. Management organizing is 'establishing and maintaining' interpersonal relations. Those little boxes that we draw and those words that we write on paper and the nice neat little job descriptions that we make — all that is wonderful except one thing — those are people! People who become ill, people who get feelings hurt, people who become offended, people who get tired, people who become depressed. If you do not like both people and people's problems, **get out of management.** If your attitude, when a problem emerges or when a person fails, is "Will these people never learn?" — it is better that you leave management to somebody else. Your attitude should be like that of the Lord Jesus to His disciples. A.B. Bruce brings this out very clearly in his book (now out of print), THE TRAINING OF THE TWELVE. He taught them the same thing over and over again. Finally they began to grasp a little bit of what He was trying to say. Establish and maintain inter-personal relationships. You must do it day after day after day. In management you never come to the place where you can say, "I am finished." You are not building a table or a chair; you are working with lives, with human beings, with minds, with emotions, with hearts, with frail bodies subect to all the pressures of an ever changing environment.

MANAGEMENT LEADING

Of all four functions, management leading is the most psychological and the least mechanical. The others admit more of a mechanical aspect than leading. When it comes to leading, we are much more involved with inter-personal relationships. Basically, management leading is the work we do to inspire and to impel people to take specific action. It involves five parts:

First, DECISION MAKING, that is, problem identification and problem solving. Decision making is the work we do to arrive at judgments and conclusions. A part of decision making is creativity or brain-storming. Decision making is not just intuitive — not just something that we do — like snapping our fingers. There is a process in which we can engage to arrive at logical judgments and conclusions. Decision making is not entirely mystical. In fact, a mystic can make some very bad judgments. The fact we are mystics does not ensure that we are going to arrive at proper judgments and conclusions always. We may arrive at very wrong judgments and conclusions.

Second, COMMUNICATING is the work in which we engage to arrive at an understanding between ourselves and other people.

Third, MOTIVATING is one of the biggest subjects on the list. This is the work we do to cause people to want to do what needs to be done.

Fourth, SELECTING PEOPLE is the work in which we engage to appraise people's God-given capacities and opportunities and to fit them with the work for which they are best suited. How many misplaced Christian workers there are!

Fifth, DEVELOPING PEOPLE has to do with the work we do to upgrade the capacities which have been given by the Holy Spirit. Here is a man who has been equipped or gifted to do something. To develop him we help enlarge those capacities, we build upon them. This is what we mean by developing people.

MANAGEMENT CONTROLLING

Management controlling has to do with four activities:

First, ESTABLISHING PERFORMANCE STANDARDS. Now, this means that we agree with the person or the persons working with us as to what quality work is going to be done, before it is begun.   There is a mutual agreement; here is the job and here is the standard to which it is going to be performed.   Right here we get into a lot of trouble.   You give a man a job or ask him to do something.   He assumes, "This is not very important.   I can do it sloppily or half-heartedly.   It does not really matter."   We, however, attach a great deal of significance to it. So, we must adequately communicate in order that we agree about the standard for the job; otherwise there is going to be incompatibility and serious friction.   Establish performance standards.   If a new missionary is assigned to you, let him know what you expect of him.   What breaches of relationships we get here!   The missionary does not know what is expected of him and you do not tell him.   He flounders and then gets frustrated and then after a while he becomes embarrassed with himself.   You become all the more irritated with him and the gulf just widens.

Second, PERFORMANCE MEASURING.   This means that whether a fellow is counting money, passing out literature on the street, planting a church in a pioneer area, or whatever he is doing, somebody is measuring his work.   Now, the point here is not how many souls he has led to Christ; it is his performance in his work, and it may or may not be reflected in souls saved.   What built-in resistance we have to this!

Third, PERFORMANCE EVALUATING is the work we do to appraise the importance of this individual's work in relation to all of the other work which is being performed in the organization, and with respect to accomplishing the total goal.   Get into this kind of thing seriously and you will find a lot of people doing jobs that do not need to be done.

Fourth, PERFORMANCE CORRECTING involves not only correcting mistakes that have been made.   It involves coaching, providing the person with the "how": saying to him, "Here is how you do it"; and then coming back to him to correct mistakes and continually providing him with methods for accomplishing his work.   You do not have to know how to do it yourself; but you have to know where to send him for the help he needs to learn how to do it.   Performance correcting includes coaching.   In other words, we do not just set standards and measures and evaluate.   We coach: "Go see him."   "Read that book."   "Take that course."   "Talk to that person."   "Read this article."

Do you see job description written on the chart?   That is not covered in so many words in the outline.   However, we will insert **Job Description** under the heading of Establishing Objectives or Organizational Structure.   It could fit in either place.   Job description is one of the most important aspects of management.   The organization, the structure, points toward the goal; the job description points toward the goal. All of the PLOC points toward the goal. The personal and departmental long-range and short-range objectives all point toward the goal. Everything we are doing is concerned with the accomplishment of these objects. (See Chart No. 1 Pages 38-39.) This is the battle we have to fight: first, to determine what the objectives are, and second, to keep pressure applied by everything and everybody for the accomplishing of those objectives.

CHAPTER II

BASIC TYPES OF ORGANIZATIONAL
ORIENTATION AND PRINCIPLES

I wish to draw your attention to something that is basic and foundational to this whole subject. There are three basic types of organizational orientation or organizational mentalities. First, there is **TASK** orientation. Task orientation says, "Do this — do that — do something else." Task orientation is primarily concerned with the performance and activity of the moment — not the distant goal. The task orientation is revealed in a little illustration that I am sure you are all acquainted with. A man walked up to several workmen.

He asked one workman, "What are you doing?"

"I'm laying bricks."

He addressed another, "What are you doing?"

"I am installing glass."

Finally, he spoke to a man who was wheeling a wheelbarrow, "What are you doing?"

"I'm building a cathedral."

All of these men had a task orientation. "Here is what we do. Here is the activity in which we are engaged." In industry the task orientation expresses itself this way: "Screw on that nut. Never mind what you are building. Just screw that nut on that bolt." The average mission has a task orientation.

There is another kind of orientation. CONTROL — the control orientation is concerned primarily with government, authority and decisions. Control orientation says the most important thing about our association is to make sure that control is maintained, that a proper form of government is perpetuated, that we do things to a certain standard. Control says it does not make any difference whether we accomplish anything or not, but let us make sure that we do it right.

Then, there is another type of orientation, GOAL orientation. Goal orientation says, "Government, authority, procedure, precedent, history, all must serve this accomplishment." Goal orientation says, "Everything that is done (task) must strategically contribute to the stated goal. Goal orientation is utterly obsessed with definitive objectives and causes everything else to be subservient to that objective. This is the hardest thing to maintain. Generally, religious organizations start out with a goal orientation, deteriorate next to a task orientation ,and then the bottom — the bitter dregs of organizational deterioration —

to control orientation. That is the stepladder down, the way we tend to go.

I have been talking about evangelical ecumenicity for a long time and have been exercised about ecumenicity within a predetermined theological framework. One day I was talking with a lady about her mission. She is the head of a certain mission. They have not had a new missionary in eight years and they are going down. They are not accomplishing anything — they are in great trouble — and yet they perpetuate their old form. They have degenerated to the bottom of a control organization. I said to her, "Dear lady, why don't you merge your mission with somebody that can bring vitality and help in the areas where you need it so that the people involved in your work can accomplish the goals to which they originally committed themselves?" "Oh, merge! We could not merge. That would be an invasion of the sanctity of the origin of our mission." What she was really saying was, "We have no goal other than the perpetuation of our form." Perpetuate she will, and perpetuate it her constituency will!

We will see this attitude when we talk about organization — sentiment versus purpose. It is a fierce battle, but all of these things move toward this goal. Everything is subservient to this. Everything! Is this Biblical? Yes, indeed — "Forgetting those things which are behind and reaching forth unto those things which are before, I press toward the mark for the prize of the high calling of God in Christ Jesus" (Phil. 3:13, 14). "What mean ye to weep and break my heart? For I am ready not to be bound only, but also to die at Jerusalem for the name of the Lord Jesus" (Acts 21:13). "I'm ready to preach" (Rom. 1:15). "He steadfastly set his face to go to Jerusalem" (Luke 9:51). It is very Biblical. I can only lay brick with one hand and wield a sword with the other, but brother, I am going to build this wall. It is our spiritual degeneration that has taken us down this bitter road to task and control orientation to the exclusion of our goal orientation. Some of us in our organizations will have a bitter struggle to ever regain this — sometimes it cannot be regained in an organization. Maybe you have heard of the inevitable trend in an organization. It starts with a **man** with a vision and a burden. Then it becomes a **movement,** and this generally degenerates into a **machine.** Then, finally, it becomes a **monument.** These are the four "M's" of organizational deterioration and it results in "control organization.' This mentality says, "Never mind whether we are doing anything; let us just make sure that we are doing it properly!"

The best way we have discovered to get things done through a group of people committed to a common objective is to have someone within the group practicing the work or doing the work of planning, leading, organizing and controlling.

The **principle of operating priority:** This teaches us that when we are called upon to perform both management and operating work during the same period, a man tends to give first priority to operating work.   Now, let me illustrate.   Here you have a group of church planters, evangelists, in a given situation, country or province.   These people, however few or many, are banded together to do church-planting.   The purpose of this organization is to evangelize with the view to establishing local operating groups of believers in this province or city.   One of these men is put in the position of chairman, manager, superintendent, director or whatever you want to call him.   This man will manage, plan, lead, organize and control — these people and all of the resources and all of the time.   Operating would be preaching, evangelizing, conducting meetings, visiting, handing out literature, making disciples, etc. Now, when this man who is skilled in operating is put in a managerial situation, and is required to both operate and manage at the same time, he will tend to give preferential priority to operating rather than to managing.

It is important to understand the difference between operating and managing.   This principle could apply to a machine shop where you have three men operating pieces of machinery.   One of them is made the manager, but he is also required to operate a machine at the same time. He will tend to let the work of management slip in deference to the operating work every time. You and I are put in positions of management. Our constant temptation is to operate rather than to manage. We will always sermonize. We will always go out and meet people and talk with people; we will do anything before we manage. And this is disastrous in its final results because it throws the group into chaos and confusion. You meet these symptoms when a man who should be managing is operating. People commonly say, "Well, I don't know what we are here for — I don't know what he is doing." People will constantly hold the other people in suspicion with respect to their activities and motives when there is lack of management. This lack of management leads to frustration and results in people casting their minds back to the "good old days when there was just Joe and Bill and me out here and we knew what we were doing. But it is all changed now." The reason is — a lack of management.

The **principle of organizational levels** teaches us that the lower the organizational level, the more operating work a manager is required to perform. Now, conversely, the higher the organizational level, the more a man is required to manage. I do not think this needs any enlargement. Where you are determines how much of your time should be spent in planning, leading, organizing and controlling. It is very interesting, though, to note that the world at large is not ready to accept management as work. We accept it as a reward for faithfulness or stature or achievement, but not work.

Someone says to me, "Mr. Hendrix, what do you do?"

"Well, I am the Director in North America for Far Eastern Gospel Crusade."

"Oh, that is fine, but what do you do?"

"Well, I plan, lead, organize and control for all of the people involved in the North America operation of Far Eastern Gospel Crusade."

"Thanks, but what do you do?"

We are not geared in our mentality to accept this as a type of work. This is why we do not require people to have training in this sphere. We do not set people aside and say, "Your job is to plan, lead, organize and control."

What if you hired a fellow to paint your house and he came with ladders, paint, and paint brushes and sat down out front and said, "Well, it needs painting all right, but I think I will drink some coffee." And he drank coffee for four hours. Then he said, "That house sure needs painting and I know I ought to paint it. Somebody has to paint it, but I think I will work in the garden. I like flowers." Well, this could be stretched on and on and on. The point is, he is not doing what he is supposed to do. Why we steer away from this work we will try to discover as we go along.

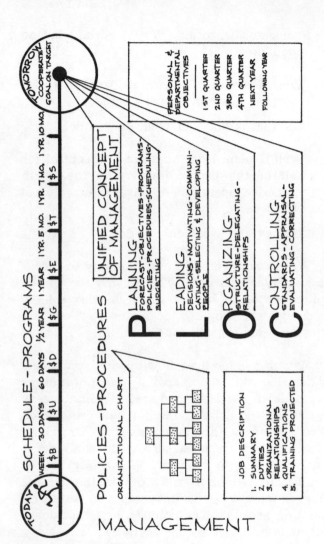

TODAY

SCHEDULE - PROGRAMS

TOMORROW
COOPERATIVE
GOAL ON TARGET

| WEEK | 30 DAYS | 60 DAYS | 1/2 YEAR | 1 YEAR | 1 YR. 5 MO. | 1 YR. 7 MO. | 1 YR. 10 MO. |
| $B | $U | $D | $G | $E | $T | $S | |

PERSONAL &
DEPARTMENTAL
OBJECTIVES

1 ST QUARTER
2 ND QUARTER
3 RD QUARTER
4 TH QUARTER
NEXT YEAR
FOLLOWING YEAR

POLICIES - PROCEDURES   UNIFIED CONCEPT OF MANAGEMENT

PLANNING
FORECAST - OBJECTIVES - PROGRAMS -
POLICIES - PROCEDURES - SCHEDULING -
BUDGETING

LEADING
DECISIONS - MOTIVATING - COMMUNI-
CATING - SELECTING & DEVELOPING
PEOPLE

ORGANIZING
STRUCTURE - DELEGATING -
RELATIONSHIPS

CONTROLLING
STANDARDS - APPRAISAL -
EVALUATING - CORRECTING

ORGANIZATIONAL CHART

JOB DESCRIPTION
1. SUMMARY
2. DUTIES
3. ORGANIZATIONAL
   RELATIONSHIPS
4. QUALIFICATIONS
5. TRAINING PROJECTED

MANAGEMENT

CHART NO. 1

CHAPTER III

PLANNING—ITS CHARACTERISTICS

Louis A. Allen in **The Management Profession** defines planning as, "The work a manager performs to pre-determine a course of action." According to him, the all-encompassing view of planning is as follows:

1. **Forecasting:** The work a manager performs to estimate the future.

2. **Establishing objectives:** The work a manager performs to determine the end results to be accomplished.

3. **Programming:** The work a manager performs to establish the sequence and priority of action-steps to be followed in reaching objectives.

4. **Scheduling:** The work a manager performs to establish a time sequence for programme steps.

5. **Budgeting:** The work a manager performs to allocate resources necessary to accomplish objectives.

6. **Procedure:** The work a manager performs to develop and apply standardized methods of performing specified work.

7. **Policies:** The work a manager performs to develop and interpret standing decisions that apply to repetitive questions and problems of significance to the enterprise as a whole.

Planning is one of the most important words in organizational functions today. Always vital in successful management, it has assumed unparalleled importance in these days of jet-swift change. Abraham Lincoln said in 1858, "If we could first know where we are, and whither we are tending, we could better judge what to do and how to do it." Follow carefully: Informed planning is based upon the fact that phenomena do not occur singly. Everything comes preceded by many others, accompanied by many and followed by many. The cause-and-effect relationship of things is the most important natural law we have. Planning, according to Fayol, the successful French coal miner, is as follows: "The plan of action is, at one and the same time, the result envisaged, the line of action to be followed, the stages to go through (that is the programme, to use Louis Allen's terminology) and the methods to use."

Why do we have such difficulty with planning? We will try to answer this question as we go along. Here is a quotation from the Vice-President of Westinghouse Company. He said,

"Today the world is changing so rapidly that we cannot train to meet a given situation. We must educate people to cope with whatever changes may occur." Here is where we have failed in missions. We have trained pastors to meet issues that we faced fifteen years ago. Those battles have been fought. We must educate people to cope with whatever changes may occur and there are only three things about the future that we are certain of:

1. It will not be like the past.

2. It will not be like we think it is going to be.

3. The rate of change will be faster than ever before.

Look again so that you can see all the components of planning. These things all fit together like a piece of fine machinery. You can take them out and examine them one at a time, but in order for a plan to work all of the things have to fit together like a piece of machinery. There are seven of them. They are listed above.

With this in mind, I want first to consider the characteristics of planning. The first characteristic is that planning consists of decisions made in advance of action. Are you aware of the tremendous problem that decision-making is for the average human being? I saw a cartoon some time ago. A girl was speeding along the road in her car and she came to a fork in the road. There was a sign in the island in the middle of the diverging roads that said, "Take either road." She ran into the post that said, "Take either road." As she climbed out of the car and spoke to the policeman the caption read, "I couldn't make up my mind which one to take." Do you know that indecisiveness is one of the greatest enemies of management? The reluctance, the hesitancy to make a decision — how many times I face this! Somebody comes and says, "I would like to talk to you about our work, our organization. We cannot get decisions. Nobody wants to decide. Everybody seeks to avoid responsibility." They say, "We have to write to New York, Chicago, London or to somewhere else to get a decision, and this demoralizes people terribly." Now, planning is difficult because planning says, "Today we are deciding many issues related to the future." Planning involves decisions made in advance of action. Nothing so reveals courageousness and direction on the part of a Christian worker like true planning. This is what God wants us to accomplish. This is the thing to which we are committed under the direction of the Holy Spirit, and here are the decisions that we are making today and we are committed in this direction. This takes real courage! It limits us. If you fire a bullet towards a bull's-eye, it is very difficult to catch up with it and change the target. Actually, we would prefer purposelessness to the choice of purpose that now commits us in a definite direction. It is easier to live with purposelessness and aimlessness than it is to live with decisions made today that commit us tomorrow and the next month and the next year.

The second characteristic of planning is that it deals with the future behaviour of people. Do not assume that the people you deal with are any different than the people that anyone else deals with in the world, in industry, in business or in another country.

Some asked me after I had been in Africa about a day and a half,

"What are your impressions about Africa?"

"Well," I said, "I have none yet except that it is like every other country I have ever been in. It is full of people!"

And this is an amazingly common denominator. In these past few years, as I have travelled and observed missions in many situations and have met missionaries who come from all over the world to the Furlough Missionary Institute in Detroit, I have been amazed. You can narrow the problems down to a small list. They are all the same in every country, and the biggest is: "We deal with people." You must not say, "Well, it is different in industry." No, it is precisely the same. I have gone to industrial management seminars. I have listened to these men in industrial settings grapple with the same problems that you and I are grappling with in our work. They ask the same questions you ask. Precisely! When we plan, we are deciding now that other people will carry out specified actions at future periods. This means we have to co-ordinate, motivate, channel, guide and communicate without fail, constantly.

One of the most important things we can learn about the future behaviour of people is found in a little slogan or catchy phrase that I want to leave with you: "T.P.A." — **Take People Action.** The principle is, "If you expect someone to co-operate with you later in doing something, involve them now in the decision to do it." Two of the most important aspects of planning, dealing with the future behaviour of people, are these: One is **conditioning.** We must condition people! Remember, management on the part of the Christian worker is never a partner to subterfuge or insincerity or anything that is the slightest bit dishonest or misrepresentative. Never! I am not suggesting anything like that. Conditioning does not mean deceiving him or hood-winking him or pulling the wool over his eyes. Conditioning means giving the person information so that he knows the facts; it means involving him in everything that you know about the situation. Do you know that people hate secretiveness on the part of a leader? Why is a man secretive? Because his ego craves to know something that somebody else does not know.

R. E. Thompson, Chairman of the Board of the Far Eastern Gospel Crusade for many years, founder of Missionary Internship, and a missionary to China, says, "Tell your people everything you can tell them and they will seldom demand that you tell them what you should not tell them. There is a place for secrets, but if you will tell your people all you can, you will seldom find them asking you to tell them what you should not tell them."

How do you go about telling? It depends upon the subject matter and the situation at hand. Some things can be adequately conveyed in a memorandum or a letter, but letters are vain vehicles for communication! The best way, of course, is face to face; but the larger the group the bigger the problem. The leader should take advantage of every opportunity with his people to condition them, and if you faithfully condition people, they will not hold it against you when you have forgotten. One of the manager's jobs is to condition people for the inevitable change that is coming down the road. God revealed His ways to Moses and His acts to the children of Israel. The man at the top must constantly be conditioning the people under him. Take every opportunity and do it every way you can.

The other aspect of dealing with the behaviour of people is timing. There is a time question — When? The immature leader always feels he has got to do it now; and if he finds he cannot do it now, he takes it as a personal affront. That is immaturity. I remember one time I had a bright idea when I was a pastor. The only problem was that it occurred to me on Monday and we were having our annual business meeting on Wednesday. So, I sprung it on the congregation! Do you know what happened? They threw it out. Because it was a bad idea? No, it was a good one. A year later they accepted the idea with no problem. What was wrong? My timing was wrong. When we are planning for the future behaviour of people, we have to both condition and time. This means that you must know well in advance definitely where you are going.

The third characteristic is that planning involves **change**. I am convinced that change is the most evident characteristic of our time and I am also convinced that the average evangelical Christian workers are oblivious to, and unmindful of, change. Some of us are living as if conditions were the same today that prevailed twenty-five years ago. We are as out of touch as we can be. We are not aware of the changes that have developed around us. The AMA President, L. Appley, in trying to describe how rapidly changes are taking place, put it this way: "We are confronted with the rate of change of change." It is no longer the rate of change — it is the rate of change of change! That is how rapidly change is taking place and it is touching you and the people you are working with, and you might think, "Oh, I am living in a country or village where change will not affect us." **Do you realize that tech-nology** has advanced more in the last fifty years than in the preceding five thousand years and that in the next five years we will double our technological advance? Very few Christian workers are able to adapt to the demands of this kind of change in society.

In January, 1967, U.S. NEWS AND WORLD REPORT made a prediction, "The Wondrous World of 1990." Some of the things that were predicted for 1990 were amazing. I have read that by 1972 there will be more people alive on the earth than have died since mankind first appeared. Some technicians are predicting that by the year 2,000 we will have instant world-wide communication. We will have continent-wide television communication. Some of the countries of the world will proudly display automated high-ways. These are already in the experimental stages. Fish will be herded and raised in off-shore pens in the ocean to feed the population. There will be automatic atomic and hydrogen controls. Drugs will alter basic personality patterns in the individual. It is amazing! Eric Hoffer in his book, THE ORDEAL OF CHANGE says, "Nobody really likes the new. We all fight change. Taking a new step, uttering a new word, is what people fear the most." And for people like you and me, the issue is **change or die.**

Do you know that in 1960 the Gallup Poll in the United States revealed that 14% of the popu-lation felt that the church in America was irrelevant and unrelated to real life situations? In 1967, the same poll showed that 54% of the population said the church was unrelated to society. We are being pressed in a corner these days to see if we are really going to adapt to meet the needs of a changing world.

What do I mean? I was conducting a week of meetings in Ocean City, New Jersey, U.S.A. (This is a seaside town in North America where people come in large crowds during the summer. They stay in the hotels and tourist homes and swim in the ocean all day.) I was preaching there for about a week. Campus Crusade, an aggressive evangelistic group, was having meetings there. They had about 60-70 students working through the summer trying to evangelize the hippies that went there. So I said to myself, "I'm going to work with these people." After the service I tried to look like a hippie. I took my tie off and pulled my shirt tail out and looked as sloppy as I could. I would slouch down the street and go to what they called their 'Hunger Hanger' — the place where they had a psychedelic picture on the window and all the rest of it. I had the time of my life.

Do you know what I found? I found a whole segment of the population that just repulsed and rejected the Church. One night two of these fellows walked into the church at the end of the meeting with their scruffy beards, smoking cigarettes and smelling unpleasantly! The hippies have something against soap and water; I do not know what it is. You could have heard a pin drop. The people were standing around in their nice clothes, staring at them. "What are they doing here?" Well, I knew the hippies, so I went to the back of the church and greeted them. "Hello, how are you?" I shook hands with them and everybody stared dumbfoundedly. "What's going on? Who are they?" Do you know who they are? They are representatives of a great segment of this world, but we just cannot adapt to them and win them to Christ.

Robert Guy, a prolific and a provocative writer on the subject of mission strategy, said, "Difficulties result when attachments proper to faith are transferred uncritically to methods of work." It is our ideological dogmatism, our theoretical unsupported assertions, that get us into trouble. We think that because something worked in another era, it is going to work in ours. But it might not work in our era at all. It depends upon whether our emphasis is task, control or goal. That is what makes the difference.

The world often perfects and improves means to uncertain or ignoble ends; the church pursues noble ends with antiquated means. As Emerson said, "Improved means to unimproved ends." That is the world. Einstein said, "Few things so characterize our day as perfection of means and confusion of goals." Change! Change anything, change everything that can be changed to accomplish our goal. Now, does this mean we change our theology? No! I am not saying that. I am saying, however, that in our planning we come up with such a commitment to a goal that we subjugate everything else to the achieving of that goal.

Why do we not plan? Why do we not make the effort that is required to establish objectives, estimate the future programme, establish budgets and procedures? What are the barriers to planning? Let me suggest that the first reason is simply that we do not know how. Some of us do not plan because we have never seen it done. Secondly, we do not plan because most of us prefer to do things than to think about them. Planning is thinking. Planning is coordinating. Planning is analyzing. Planning is communicating. Planning is inter-acting. Planning is revising, appraising, criticizing, and it is easier to do it than it is to think about it. Thirdly, the barrier to planning is the uncertainty of the future. We do not know what tomorrow is going to be like. So we tend just to say, "Oh, what is the use? Every time I make plans they go astray. So I am just not going to try to plan any more." That is an immature attitude and it reveals a task-orientation rather than a goal-orientation. Goal-orientation will continually say, "Here is the thing we are committed to achieve." We have to keep revising and regrouping and bringing pressures to bear so that all of the activities aim toward the goal.

CHAPTER IV

PLANNING — ITS PRINCIPLES

Principle number one: **the principle of present choice** teaches us that current decisions limit future action. What does this mean? Let us suppose that a missionary organization is about to go into a certain country or a certain province and we decide the goal in this endeavour is church planting. That is our goal. We become more definite and we say that within five years we want churches started in these centres; within ten years, this many churches in these particular centres, etc. Did you hear about the old independent missionary not associated with any board, working in South America?

Someone said to him, "What is your mission strategy?"

He said, "Strategy? Well, I just travel around the countryside until I find where the Holy Spirit is working and I join Him."

I like that! That is good mission strategy. But in planning, we trust the Lord for guidance in advance. Now, we are going to go in, and we are all agreed. There is mutual commitment that this is our goal, but after we get in there we find that these poor people do not know how to read and write.   Are we going to have some literacy work?   Then we find that these people are ill. Are we going to have some medical work?   Then after a while we find that these people are hungry. They need some aid in agricultural development. Are we going to have some agricultural mission-aries come in?   Are we going to predetermine our goal in advance or are we to proliferate our activities after we are in, oftentimes to the weakening of all our purposes?   What determines our goals? Is it need?

One of our missionaries in children's work had a classic example of this.   She was working alongside two or three couples in an area in Japan, and soon after she got involved in the children's work she found that in the wintertime all the children coming to the meetings had runny noses.   So she would wipe their noses.   Well, she found that all she was doing was wiping noses! Finally, she decided, "My goal is not to see that they have clean noses.   My goal in these thirty or forty minutes that I have these children is to teach them something they will never forget from the Word of God."   So she let their noses drip.

What determines what we are going to do? Necessity?   Or are we going to make decisions now that will limit future action?   This is why planning is difficult.   This is one of the aspects of planning.   Once we get into the thing we will

find many other noble purposes which may or
may not be of God. The fact that they are noble,
the fact that they are needful activities, does not
necessarily mean that we are qualified to get involved in them. Sometimes we proliferate our
activities to the weakening of our main purposes.
I am not saying that this is right and these are
wrong. This might be right and all the rest be
wrong. That is beside the point. In planning
we have to determine in advance.

Principle number two: **the principle of positive action** teaches us that the probability of a
future event occurring increases as effort is applied systematically toward its realization. We
have X number of people, X number of hours,
and X amount of money. Our resources are
limited, and we must not have them dispersed.
This is what I meant about proliferating our
activities to the weakening of our purpose. This
is why you must say, "We want a ditch dug from
A to B." Instead we say, "All right. All of you
as you feel led, dig the ditch." That is ridiculous!

We have such a goal commitment, a goal
understanding, that we are drawn together in the
accomplishment. I get it from the missionary's
point of view and from the candidate's point of
view. This is our problem. We go home and
we say our job is church planting or evangelizing.
Then we come here and there are 1,000 (slight
exaggeration!) other activities that people are
pressured into, to the exclusion of the thing we

preach and talk about. The point is, are we so orientated to the goal that we will evaluate these other pressing needs critically?

When I saw the hunger and desperation of the Indian people, particularly the children, I was overwhelmed and crushed. I said to a group there, "In God's name how can you live and work with these people literally starving to death on your door step?" An Indian gave a good reply. He said, "We cannot do everything. The most important thing is the saving of souls. If we merely feed a man, he will get hungry again at the end of the day or week, but if we preach Jesus Christ to him, we might be able to save him from hell."

That is goal-orientation on the part of an Indian. I just turned my head and said, "Oh God, help me to have that kind of evangelistic goal-orientation." I find that most Christian organizations are so diversified in their activities that they are ineffective in everything. We have an exaggerated concept about our abilities and resources and an undisciplined approach to our task. One mission executive put down in his goals for his organization: "Our goal is to evangelize the whole world." What an exaggerated concept of his abilities and resources!

Principle number three: **the principle of commensurate effort.** This teaches us that effort applied should be commensurate with or proportionate to the results desired. If we could just grasp hold of that one thing, what a difference it could make in our ministry. But again, it presupposes an identity of goal and a commitment to that goal. It critically looks at everything you are doing and says, Here is the goal to which I am committing myself. But we are so subjective that we cannot evaluate this sort of thing critically.

Principle number four: **the principle of planning stability.** This teaches us that the stability of a plan tends to vary inversely with its extension. This means that I can plan very accurately for a week, with less accuracy for a month, with even less accuracy for a year, with even less accuracy as the time is extended. What does this mean in regard to planning? Does it mean that because of the uncertainty of the future and because of the instability of the lengthening of the plan, that I should not plan? No, it makes planning all the more imperative. Also, it means that I will constantly up-date my plan. Planning is a continuing work.

Principle number five: **the greater the departure of planned changes from present ways, the greater the potential resistance by the people involved.** Do you know who resists change? You and I resist change. And it is perhaps true that the older we are the more we resist it, but this is not necessarily true. The more insecure we are, the more we resist change. Provincialism contributes to resistance to change. We have to anticipate resistance to change and we cannot scold our people when they resist change. Some pastors I have talked to do not have a good word to say for their congregation — "These people resist everything that is new and innovative." Let us appreciate the fact that we resist change, that we do not want someone coming in and imposing something new upon us. If we realize this about ourselves it will help us to realize it about other people.

Now in the sixth place, **future events tend to result from current and past occurrences.** This is self-explanatory.

CHAPTER V

THE ESTABLISHING OF OBJECTIVES

Now we turn our attention to one of the very important components of planning. In a previous chapter we defined the various components of planning, beginning with the work of estimating the future or forecasting the future and going down through programmes, policies, budgets, schedules, etc. One of the most important aspects of planning — in fact, a component just completely inseparable from the very concept of planning — is the establishing of objectives. We must understand what our objectives are. We must be able to articulate them. They must be in written form. They must be widely displayed. People must have access to them. The people within our organization must be committed to them. They must know what they are.

To a very large degree, the effectiveness of our corporate efforts in any human enterprise depends upon our ability to concisely articulate our objectives, and the degree to which we are corporately enthusiastic about these objectives. In international organizations and operations, like missions, we get into all kinds of trouble. A frequent complaint I have heard from new missionaries and from older ones that can remember the frustrations of their earlier years is, "Well, I am not doing what I came out here to do. I am not engaged in the kind of work that was described to me when I was in seminary." I know the arguments. But still there is this basic frustration. On the one hand we visualize our purposes as such and such and then when we get to the field we find that we are involved in something altogether different. Then the argument becomes pious: "Well, look Joe, you've got to do what the Lord leads you to do." We have magnificent illustrations to show the virtues of capitulating to the pressure. It is not up to us to prove other people's spirituality. That is not what God has called us to do. God has called us to accomplish His purposes on the earth. He can take care of proving a man's spirituality without contriving circumstances to prove what a man is made of.

The problem really is, What is our objective? Frequently when you talk to people from the same organization, you get two sets of answers. This is the problem that we are faced with. I am not concerned what your objectives are, but I am concerned that you know what they are and that people with whom you work know what they are. I am concerned that everything possible be directed toward the accomplishing of those objectives, regardless of what they are.

I came upon a very interesting article in a daily devotional magazine some time ago that speaks eloquently on this subject of objectives. A newly-hired travelling salesman wrote his first report to the home office. It stunned the executives in the sales department because it was obvious that the "new help" was completely illiterate. This is what he wrote: "I seen this outfit which they never bought a dime's worth of nothin' from us and I sole them some goods. I am now going to Chicawgo." Before the services of the illiterate could be terminated by the sales manager, this letter came from Chicago, "I come here and sole them haff a millyon." Fearful if he did and afraid if he did not fire the illiterate, the sales manager dumped the problem in the lap of the president. The following morning the executives and office personnel were amazed to see a memo from the president posted on the bulletin board with the two letters written by the ignorant salesman. It read like this: "We've ben spendin' too much time tryin' to spel instead of tryin' to sel. Let's watch those sails. I want everybody should read these letters from Gootch who is on the road doin' a grate job for us and you should go out and do like he done." We should find out what we are supposed to do, and then do it.

One day I was showing a visitor around a church which had about 2,000 people in attendance. It was pastored by a friend of mine and had the oddest kind of arrangement you would ever want to see. I was showing this fellow around and explaining how this works and how that works. It is the most unconventional set-up, and my

friend said, "Somebody ought to tell this pastor
this will not work." Well, the only problem is,
it does work; he is accomplishing his objectives.

Earlier I said that everything should be
directed toward the accomplishment of our objectives. Our organizational structure should lend
itself constantly to the accomplishment of our
objectives. Our policies should insure the accomplishment of our objectives. Precedent and what
we learn from history should indicate to us how
to accomplish our objectives. The problem most
of the time is we do not really know what our
objectives are. Lorne Sanny, the successor to
Dawson Trotman in the Navigator movement, is
a sharp and creative manager. He was not always
so. After his succession to the leadership, Lorne
went through a very difficult period, and it was
only after he came upon a little booklet entitled
MANAGEMENT, written by the President of the
National Bank of Detroit, that he began to see
that here were some skills that he could acquire.
After studying the subject of management for a
number of years, Lorne Sanny came up with four
questions relative to objectives. He came upon
these questions because he found that he had to
have some point of contact with the people who
were serving under him. These four questions
are four of the most perceptive objective–oriented
questions I have ever seen.

Sanny says, "There are four things I always
ask people who come in for an interview, the

people who report to me — for whom I am responsible. First, I want to know definitively what are your objectives? You start working on this and it will revolutionize your life. Ask this question about the next sermon you are going to preach. What are my objectives in delivering this sermon? What are my objectives in having this business meeting? What are my objectives in having this interview with this person?" Lorne's first question is — WHAT ARE YOUR OBJECTIVES?

His second question is — WHAT ARE YOUR OPPORTUNITIES or what are your open doors?

His third question is, WHAT ARE YOUR RESOURCES? Here we must be realistic, not mystic. Do not spiritualize where God demands a practical outlook. Do not become spiritually evasive where God demands pragmatism. What are my resources? How many men have I got? How many hours have I got? How much money have I got? How many cars have I got? How many tents have I got? How much literature have I got?

The fourth question has to do with strategy and then it just goes back up the list from the bottom to the top. WHAT IS YOUR STRATEGY FOR APPLYING YOUR RESOURCES TO YOUR OPPORTUNITIES TO OBTAIN YOUR OBJECTIVES? This will force a man to think creatively. This removes the responsibility from the manager to devise all the steps to be taken, and thrusts the creative responsibility upon the individuals themselves.

Goals have a powerful effect. Objectives clearly articulated and mutually agreed upon in a group have a powerful effect. This more than anything else explains the supreme accomplishments of new organizations. Have you ever watched a new organization emerge and accomplish so much? Probably some of you reminisce about the old days of your organization when you accomplished so much. Now, of course, we tend to distort the past. We tend to remember only the good about the past and forget the bad. Someone has said, There are only two good places to be: the place where you have just been and the place where you are going. We normally can only look realistically at the moment, but nonetheless it is a fact that usually new organizations are highly goal–oriented or objective–oriented and everything is subservient to the goal. This need not be exclusively a characteristic of the new or recently-emerged organization. It can be a continuing characteristic of any organization if we want it to be and if we are willing to make it so at all costs.

Let us see the powerful effect of clear objectives. Most good work in management is problematic; that is, it aims at accomplishing some specific end, some goal, or it aims at achieving some terminal point. The definition of these objectives for the whole organization, for all subordinate organizations, and for individuals in it, is the logical starting place for management improvement. This is important. Many old, staid, ponderous, slow-moving organizations can be rejuvenated to a goal orientation. Many cannot. If it is possible, then it is possible only as we make an attack on this subject of objectives. I hope you do not think I am belabouring the point. I have observed that every book you read on the subject of management says the same thing. This is where we have to start: the objective for the total organization. Put this in a pyramid form. The top piece would be the objective of the total organization. Everything underneath this, every subordinate organization, must likewise be committed in this direction, though it will have goals all its own. This applies to the individual also. Every individual within this organization must have goals that are welded into the main objectives.

There are four effects of clear objectives:

1.   If you do not have a goal, then any road will get you there. The absence of a goal justifies almost any activity espoused by an individual under the guise of "This is my burden, or this is my calling, or this is the Lord's leading." I do not mean to minimize this nor speak lightly of holy things. But I think there is more evasiveness on this than most of us in Christian work are willing to admit, and it is tragic.

2. You cannot measure results without some prior expectation against which to judge them. In other words, if you do not have clear objectives, then almost any level or degree or quality of performance will satisfy the people involved. Almost any activity can be justified on an individualistic basis. This is where we are in missions and in our churches. We do it very spiritually: "The Lord led me." "This is my burden." So off we go.

There are some people who will never work in an organization. If we were able to devise an ideal organization, some people would never fit into it. Let us accommodate these people outside organizational structures. Let us recognize that not everyone can conform to an organizational structure. If there is an individual who must work on his own, let him go. The great bulk of humanity, however, needs this kind of restraining and control.

3. If you are not clear on your objectives, you do not know when things are drifting. You do not realize it until a lifetime has been spent and then, suddenly, it dawns upon you, "I didn't achieve it. I didn't hit it." Oh, we rationalize, we exonerate ourselves, we excuse ourselves, we make allowances; but we fail.

4. People in an organization cannot perform with maximum effectiveness if they are unaware of the goals, the purposes of their work, or how

well they are doing in relation to the goals. You who are in supervisory responsibilities, do you know the three main problems with respect to missionaries? The first is, What is my job? The second one is, How am I doing? How well are they doing in relation to those goals? I have talked with scores of missionaries who have spent a term on the field and have not known until they were ready to go home and had a pre-furlough interview how they were doing! One reason we fail to tell people how they are doing is that some of us in responsible positions are scared. We are insecure ourselves. We do not have, and have not trusted the Holy Spirit to give us, the courage to face a man and tell him how he is doing. Next, Where do I go for help? People want help. People need help. If we want to have effective management situations we will build into our situations these avenues whereby people can obtain help.

"Look, I'm having trouble with my wife and children. Where do I go for help?"

"I'm having problems with the local or na-
X tional church. Where do I go for help?"

"I'm having problems in my own mind with some theological questions. Where do I get help? Is there a person or a group or something to which I could go for help?"

A good manager will establish a relationship with his men so that they will gladly come and say, "I need some help. Can you tell me what to do?"

In articulating these goals, we prepare our-selves with a very basic foundation for all of our future performance. Goals are not always ad-hered to with equal enthusiasm by every member of the organization. People deeply committed come in but they become disillusioned and need to be constantly reminded of the goals of the organization. We must constantly be re-oriented to the goal week after week, year after year.

Now the question comes: "How do we es-tablish goals?" First of all, there are two types of goals — the long-range and short-range goals. Normally we think of long-range goals running from five years onward. Anything less than that becomes short-range. How do we go about es-tablishing these goals? Do we start at the goal end of the chart and work back or do we start here where we are and work forward? (See Chart No. 1, Pages 38-39.) This is the hardest work you will ever engage in. It is easy to write down what you think ought to be done. How-ever, when it involves twenty, thirty, fifty or a hundred people, then it is difficult. We start with the ultimate goal. What do we want to accom-plish ultimately? For example, this could be to build cathedrals in every metropolitan centre in Africa. We must determine what the goal is and then work back this way (toward "today" on the chart). Determining this is the biggest job. It becomes relatively easy to determine short-range goals.

The difficulty comes when you begin moving in that direction. Suppose we encounter obstacles. When we do, the temptation is to veer off to a lesser, more intermediate goal. For example, the goal is the formation of churches in a hitherto unreached area in Africa. That is what we want to accomplish. Most of us have this weighing heaviest on our hearts. When we start in that direction, we are going to meet all kinds of obstacles. We have to watch that we do not veer off and become satisfied with a lesser and intermediate goal. Management is concerned with applying the pressure to get back on course, heading for the target. You have read how missiles work. Do you know that the basic function of the guidance system of a rocket is, first of all, to determine the goal or the target and then to feed back to the earth at a guidance centre or computer the detailed, minute information that will tell the operators of the machinery if there is the slightest veering off? In other words, they do not wait to correct it; they act immediately. When there is the slightest veering off, a computer must know it and the missile must be pushed back up on course. You must know **now** if you are off course. This is the concern of management. Management is not concerned with dominating another human personality, nor with asserting itself, nor with the acquiring and attaining of a status. Management is concerned with what? Objectives. This is why you must have management.

What happens when you do not have management? You veer off the course. Not only that, if you do not have management when you veer off, what happens to all your people that are involved? What is the result in the minds of these people? Confusion, loss of confidence, and frustrations!

The emotion I observe most in Christian work is frustration. It is not frustration because people are not responding to the gospel and being saved. Any Biblically—oriented person has an answer to that kind of devilish frustration. It is frustration resulting from a lack of management within our human enterprise. This is our trouble. Management says, "We are off course; let us with our resources get back on target." I have been in countries where the missionaries are suffering all sorts of hardships. I have been in some of those tribal situations in southeast Asia, in Thailand, in Viet Nam, in Cambodia, where missionaries live in tremendously primitive situations. Some of you have lived and worked there. Missionaries are not frustrated by this. I have seen national pastors working in situations in Cambodia, where they could not hand out a piece of literature without a permit from a police officer. I have known of pastors who have had their wives imprisoned because they allegedly gave out a piece of literature without permission, but these pastors have been absolutely radiant in the face of that kind of persecution. Yet because of lack of management they have been in absolute bondage and defeat. This could be different if we simply recognized some of these skills and acquired them.

Here are five rules for establishing objectives. Number one: Consider past performance. Number two: Set realistic levels. Goals must be realistic, not ethereal, nor the product of a wild imagination, but achievable. Number three: State objectives in measurable terms. Number four: Build in an improvement factor in goal setting. Goals must challenge. Men are made to be stretched. Have you ever got the feeling, "Oh, I would like to find myself a quiet little village where there are no telephones, no one to disturb me, and just sit down and let the rest of the world go by?" Do you know how long that would last? For most of us, a very short time. My wife refuses to go on a vacation unless I have a briefcase full of books and some papers that I am working on, or people I am going to see, or sermons I am going to preach. She says, "I'm not going to go and sit down somewhere with you. You'll go mad!" "I count not myself to have apprehended, but this one thing I do . . ." I put myself on that stretching, torturing device to apprehend that for which I have been laid hold of by Jesus Christ. That is human nature. Build in an improvement factor. Number five: I have

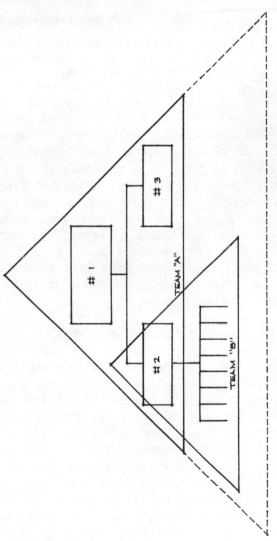

PYRAMID WITHIN A PYRAMID

NUMBERS ONE, TWO & THREE MAKE UP TEAM "A"; THEN MAN #2 ALONG WITH HIS SUBORDINATES MAKE UP TEAM "B"; #2 BECOMES THE LINK BETWEEN THE 2 TEAMS.

already mentioned this — T.P.A. — "Take People Action."

There is another aspect that should be mentioned. That is, the difference between corporate goals — the total goal of all the association of human beings — and the lesser individual goals. There is a distinction. We cannot adequately determine individual goals until we have determined corporate goals. You must have the same relationship between corporate goals and individual goals that you have between long-range and short-range goals. You start with your long-range goals and work back. Likewise you start with your corporate goals and then you begin to work in your departmental goals, your divisional goals, your project goals, your institutional goals and your individual goals.

Within the pyramid there may be other pyramids. If the goal is the planting of churches in Africa in hitherto unreached pioneer areas, you may have a large project, e.g. a hospital, and within this you would have another pyramid and the same situation would prevail. Within that pyramid there could be other pyramids, depending upon how large this organization is. Individuals would be related in these situations as well as in the overall picture. All of these activities move toward the ultimate goal. It is this concept that makes the difference between success and failure. A strong natural leader instinctively, by virtue of his dynamic personality, accomplishes this sort of thing. In a very natural way, almost totally psychologically, he achieves the goal very effectively. But in the absence of such a man the articulation of objectives and the adherence to those objectives can do the same thing.

I hope you see the difference between long-range and short-range goals, between corporate and individual goals. Therefore, let your prime target be the determination of your objectives. What is your group trying to accomplish? Assuming that we have established objectives and that we have satisfactorily taken people action and our people are committed to the stated goals, the next thing to do is to organize for this particular function.

CHAPTER VI

ORGANIZING

In a recent issue of U.S. News and World Report there was this interesting story about a British military team trying to cut down on the manpower used in handling a field cannon. Always there had been six men assigned to each cannon but there were only five jobs. The men studied each job and went to the instruction manual. From the first edition on, every manual called for a crew of six. Finally, they located the man who had written the manual originally, a retired general, and they asked him what the sixth man was supposed to do. He replied, "The sixth man? He holds the horses." They had not used horses for many, many years, but the job persisted. No reason was necessary; precedent becomes reason enough!

If our objective is clearly defined and if we are convinced that it is of God and committed to it, the people involved in the organization will accept it as God's assignment. It is necessary to devise an organizational structure which in itself will achieve the objectives.

Firstly, a definition of management organizing. This is the grouping and arranging and relating of the work to be performed, necessary

for a group of people to accomplish the goal
effectively. The little blocks in the organizational
chart do not represent status nor salary levels.
They identify and relate work to be performed
which is necessary in order to accomplish the
organizational goals.

Here is a quotation: "A manager in managing
must develop an organization capable of accomplishing its objectives." What things might happen
which would indicate the need for alteration of
the structure? A change of goal would neces-
sitate a change here. How about a change in
the capacities of the people involved? How about
a change in the environment in which we are
trying to accomplish this goal? All these will
affect the organizational structures. Twenty-five
years or so ago in the U.S.A. Sunday evening
services became very popular. This was a way
to reach the unconverted. They did not have
anywhere else to go so they went to church on
Sunday night. They did not go Sunday morning
because they slept in, but they went on Sunday
night. They did not have television to watch nor
have so many cars then to race around the country
as they do now. If you get any unconverted people
into a church today it is on Sunday morning,
certainly not on Sunday night. Yet how many
churches doggedly persist in having a Sunday
evening evangelistic service? We refuse to accept
the changes dictated by an evolution in our environment. What happens? We have task-orientation!

Alvin Brown says, "Organization defines the part which each member of an enterprise is expected to perform and the relations between such members to the end that their concerted effort or endeavour shall be most effective for the purpose of the enterprise."

Mooney and Riley describe organization as "the form of every human association for the attainment of a common purpose."

General Foods defines organization as the plan by which a group of people pool their efforts toward designated objectives through definition and division of activities, responsibilities and authority. Why do we give a man this job and give him this authority and allow him to make these kinds of decisions? Because together that is the best way to accomplish the goal.

Overloaded! is the cry of the average Christian worker. Most Christian workers are not overworked; they are under-motivated. However, overload which directly affects operating efficiency may stem from poor organization, and in some cases the work itself may be too unrelated for effective performance. What should we do?

One thing to consider is the possibility of eliminating some of our objectives in order better to accomplish a more restricted list of objectives. Many missionary societies find this hard to accept, especially where they attach such significance to precedent and to the way they have done things for the last hundred years or so.

Secondly, the implication of organizational dynamics. The simple fact is that organizations are made up of people. People change, environments change, the demands upon an organization are constantly changing from day to day. This means that the people within the organization must be willing to have their structure and their activities altered to accomplish the goal. The organization, like a human being, must develop. I am sure that you have used as an illustration of spiritual development the tragedy of a physically under-developed person. Some years ago I saw one of the most sickening things I have ever seen in my life — a boy in his teens chronologically who was mentally two. He was almost a vegetable. What a tragedy! Well, this occurs organizationally too. Where organizations are brought into existence, people go along effectively for a short time, only to degenerate while their environment moves an ahead of them and they just stay bogged down and entangled and do not develop. Organization must live and breathe, develop and grow and change.

My seventeen-year-old son comes and says, "Dad, may I borrow the car tonight?" And my wife says, "Oh, my baby, my baby, my baby . . ." I tell her, "My dear, he's no baby. Look at him! He's a six footer." But she cannot think of her son as anything but Mama's baby. Of course, she is glad that he is growing and developing, but that kind of growth and development must take place within an organization. In the physical development, the criterion by which we measure normality is the relationship of that individual to others. However, the criterion by which we measure organizational normality is the achievement of goals. Briefly and succinctly, the implications of organizational dynamics are: growth, development and maturity.

In the third place, there is purpose versus sentimentality in Christian organizations. In the business world not all businesses are highly successful and well organized. It would amaze you to know how many people in business study management but go away and never do anything about it. However, business has one advantage that we do not have in Christian work — what we call P & L, a profit and loss statement. If a business does not show a profit, and if over a long period it continues to show a loss, somebody complains — usually the stockholders. Why? They want a return on their investment. Not only do they want a return on their investment, they want protection for their capital and the greatest protection of that capital is the continuing functioning of that organization to accomplish its goals. They want to make money on the money they have invested. If they do not see this happening on the P & L regularly, they complain loudly. But unfortunately, we do not have this in Christian work. We can sink into unbelievable organizational ineffectiveness and nobody will say anything. If they do say something they do not say it very loudly, or else somebody cries, "Oh, you're touching the Lord's anointed," or, "You're fighting against God," or, "Didn't God bring this organization into existence?" We say, "Because it has been this way, it must be right." That is tragic! It does not make much sense, but we do it anyway, and along we go. What is it then that perpetuates the organization? I think it is sentimentality.

We had a very serious situation in a church in which I once served. In fact, it was the most serious situation I have ever been confronted with in my ministerial career. A well-meaning but sticky sentimentalist said in a deacon's meeting one night, "Friends, my advice is not to touch the situation. Let's maintain peace." Well, there is a time when silence is not golden: it is yellow cowardice. There is a time when we sweep aside this kind of peacefulness and sentimentality in order to accomplish our objectives. Do you know that in the church, purposefulness is always considered eccentric, always kind of coming at the status quo from the flank? And yet, it is this kind of purposefulness to which God has called us. But we prefer to perpetuate the form on the basis of sentimentality rather than to insist upon accomplishing our purpose. Why? Well, it is more peaceful this way and we can just settle down in these little things and go through the motions without really accomplishing anything.

Some of us may be so bogged down in sentimentality that our organization does not have a chance for renewal and adaptation to the accomplishing of our purpose. If that is the case, it is tragic! Our donors or church members do not help. They feed the evil root of sentimentality rather than holding us to the highest and saying: "Now, look, are you sure that it is necessary for you to be in Africa? Are you sure that what you are doing is essential? Can you justify your being there?" Your donors will not say that. They will pat you on the head and give you another love offering. An awesome responsibility rests upon us to evaluate ourselves and to develop a goal orientation.

CHAPTER VII

THE TWO BASIC GROUPS

The next subject is an analysis of the two basic types of groups or mentalities that prevail in the two extremes of group situations. The first type of group is the **centric group.** The centric group is an association of people — religious, educational, social, or industrial, in which the general level of personal concern is greater than the general level of group concern. The result is an introspection, a turning in upon the group itself.

With the centric group there is an incompatability of objectives. Where there is an ingrown aspect, the people involved tend to give primacy to their own objectives rather than the objectives of the group. Not only that, there is resistance to authority in the centric group. The centric group is generally control-oriented. Everyone is demanding to be heard and the centric group turns on itself with a primary consideration to this question — "Are we structured so that everyone can have his say?"

I am not advocating any form of government. Every form of government can degenerate to a centric group and any form of government can be a goal-oriented group. There is a resistance to authority and lack of uniformity. While this group is always looking in on itself, it is never looking critically with regard to performance but always looking critically with regard to control. "Are we giving every man a right to say all that he feels?"

A mission organization that is centric in its association and functions from a group point of view is generally made up of mature people. Alone they are spiritually responsible, imaginative, poised and disciplined. But in a group situation all of these aspects of the centric group come to the fore. Why? I do not understand it, but I know that there is something about an association of people on certain topics that tends toward the centric aspect. Generally it is government, and it revolves around a question of decision-making or authority.

There is another type of group — the **radic group.** This is the group in which the level of group concern is greater than the general level of personal concern. Do not assume that one is secular and the other is sacred. That is not necessarily true. Some of the most radic groups I know are utterly secular. For example, the U.S. Peace Corps. A lot of the humanitarian enterprises of the world are quite radic. The point is that this group tends to radiate out rather than turn in. In this group you have goal-orientation and perceptive team work. This is the type of group that Jesus Christ designed in both the apostolate and in the Church in its growth and development. The Church was always to be a radic group, and it is a sign of our degeneracy when we become a centric group. In some of our minds, the Church exists in order to perpetuate its existence. The Church should exist in order to accomplish the goals its Lord has put before it. Quite a difference! Do we exist to perpetuate our existence? That is centric. Do we exist to accomplish our Lord's goal? That is radic. Generally, a group starts out radic and degenerates to centric. The extent to which we have become centric is the extent to which we have passed down the line through a work-orientation or a task-orientation to the bitter dregs of a control-orientation.

Management is not teaching somebody else something. Management is assimilating knowledge and beginning to demonstrate it and infecting people with it. This must be our strategy — not, "What can I teach this guy in order to set him right?" but, "What can I learn to demonstrate in my managerial post that will become nuclear or central in its growth?" Centric groups do not grow appreciably. Centric groups tend to stagnate, if not in the assimilation of new personnel, at least in the dynamics of their activity. Particularly this is true in religion because in religious types of work, we will always attract some people. What I am trying to do is to identify principles. The chief danger for the radic group is in becoming so fragmented in its purposes that dif-

ferent groups and different individuals have different purposes and they begin to compete. This
will always lead back into a centric group. It is
not that any group is solidly radic. One aspect
or the other tends to dominate. Does the goal
still grip us? Is it still worthy of our commitment?
The danger here is to have one thing in writing
and another thing in practice. That is where we
create this dichotomy, a Dr. Jekyll and Mr. Hyde.
We say our goal is one thing but actual practice
goes in another direction.

It is much easier to train a group to function
in accordance with a predescribed plan of conformity than it is to train a group to achieve a
goal. I may say to my boy, "Now do this. No,
you may not do that. Yes, do that. That's fine."
That is easier to say than, "Now, look, young
man, you are to conduct yourself in an honourable,
upright way so that at the end of your life you
will be able to say, 'I have lived honourably and
decently.' " To train him is much more difficult
than just simply saying it.

What holds the radic group together? It is
the goal. The more we are obsessed with the
goal, the more we are willing to tolerate individual
differences within the organization. The less we
are obsessed with the goal, the more we need to
have personality conformity within the organization. Somebody comes to you and he does not
say things just right. If we are goal-oriented we
say, "This man has something to contribute and

we will endure much from him because he is
going to help us reach our goal." The breadth
of tolerance in the radic group is much greater
than the breadth of tolerance in the centric group.
Precept is the greatest teacher. "We produce
after our kind." A strong goal-oriented mission
will tend to reproduce a strong goal-oriented
church and a strong goal-oriented young people's
movement within that church. The same principle
applies. You have to start where you are, with
the group you associate with. You cannot walk
into another group, to which you are not responsible for leadership and direction, and say, "Here's
how this ought to be done." These principles
apply to a multiple group just as they do to a
single group.

There is another important phase of organization to cover: the two basic types of organizational structure. These are single-man rule and
team rule.

Religious organizations come into existence
and function best initially as a single-man rule.
This is generally true but not always the case.
The man with the burden gets the job. The man
with the vision makes a decision. He is the
person who has attracted men around him. He
initiates a one-man rule. A dictatorship, whether
it is in a religious environment or in a political
situation, is always the most efficient form of
government. If you have a benevolent dictator,
you are in business. The problem is that dictators

tend to become self-centered — even in religious situations. What is the alternative to a one-man rule? The issue here is DECISION-MAKING. Who decides what this person is going to do? How much money is he going to spend? Where is he going to work? Which house is he going to live in?

The alternative to this man making all the decisions (This is in a spectrum — there could be all sorts of intermediate positions) is team work, multiple-man rule. I do not mean that the alternative to one man making all the decisions is everybody making the decisions. That is compounding the red tape which must be gone through in order to arrive at a decision. But the other alternative to one man deciding everything is to let everybody make what decisions they can in keeping with the information they have at hand and the competency they possess. In other words, decisions should always be pushed down the organizational chart. If you must err, err in asking a man to make too many decisions rather than in not asking him to make enough decisions.

Decisions should be made on the lowest possible level. Decisions should always be made as near as possible to where the work is actually performed. Unless a one-man ruler is tremendously goal-orientated, he will make as many decisions as he possibly can. Even a pastor, unless he is tremendously goal-oriented, will grasp for as much decision-making as he possibly can get. Why? To protect himself, and to be more comfortable. The only alternative I know of to insure that this man will constantly push decisions down is goal-orientation. Otherwise, our very nature will cause us to accumulate things at the top. This retards the progress of the whole group by forcing everything to be channeled through one man and that makes him feel tremendously important. But what does it do to the goal? We achieve goals best when people are allowed to make as many decisions as possible which affect their work. Let your aim be to push decision-making down.

If the group is not committed to the goal, you might as well fall back and re-group. This assumes that a leader is constantly going to be training his people how to make decisions, not how to screw nuts on bolts!

One of the men who reports to me came in some time ago. He had a thorny situation and he said, "What shall I do?"

"Let's discuss the facts," I said.

He laid the whole thing out before me, and I made some observations and asked some questions. We talked for some time about the problem.

"All right," he said, "What do you want me to do?"

I said, "This is your decision. I want you to make the decision. What do you want to do about it?"

It was important enough that I felt I had to know what the decision was, but he made the decision. I did not precisely agree. There were a couple of things I thought should be different, but they were not big enough for me to say, "Change that." I let him make his decision. That man grew a foot taller. If I had thought his decision was radically wrong, I would have explained why and I would have asked him to reconsider it. Any man who cannot train decision-making capacities in the men under him is not worthy of being in a managerial situation. The man at the top must make decisions that are major, that affect the overall situation or interpretation of policy.

There was a general in World War II whose fellow commanding officers got together and said, "We think such and such an attack ought to be made." The general said, "No, it won't work. We will lose too many men. Here is why it will not work." They considered. They over-rode this man who had to command his own men. They said, "Our decision is, we attack this way." He said, "I disagree. These are my men, and we are going to lose." They replied, "This is what we're going to do anyway." He yielded and sure enough his predictions were right. He lost many men. His own subordinate officers came back and asked, "Why?" The general said, "Our decision was . . ." and he never once indicated that he had differed. It is the absence of this kind of courage that causes friction in churches and mission groups. If you do not agree with what "they" say, are you going to go along? What alternative do you have? The alternative is to split the thing and to set "your" people at variance with the group. You can create your own little domain if that is what you want, or you can get out. The stronger the goal-orientation, the stronger a leader will strive for cohesiveness. The less the goal-orientation, the more content a leader will be to develop his own little domain. How do you build manliness or courage? I really do not know except to develop it yourself and hope it will rub off on the person that is watching you. I think the more important the goal is to us, the more courageous we are to try to achieve it. How many men does it take to ruin an organization? One man strategically placed can ruin the whole thing.

Let us make a distinction. If a man comes to me and says, "I want to talk to you personally and confidentially," that is no problem. But if he wants to talk to me personally and confidentially about the work, there can be no such thing as a personal and confidential conversation because it involves others. If it is a problem in his own life and his own family situation, that is personal. But if it involves a group goal, it is no longer personal. Tell people everything you can and you will seldom be called upon to tell them anything you should not. If they know you are open and not secretive, they will not suspect you of withholding information.

Chapter VIII

MANAGEMENT ORGANIZING PRINCIPLES

You probably have noticed that the four major functions of management have listed under them all of the principles that apply to those major headings as well as to the components. For example, under management organizing principles are the principles of organizing; also, the developing of the structure, the maintaining of relationships, and delegation. Let us look at these management organizing principles which relate to organizing as a whole, to the developing of the structure, to the work of delegation and to the work of establishing and maintaining relationships.

1. **The principle of the objective.** The organizational structure should be designed to accomplish established objectives. It follows from this that when the organizational structure no longer accomplishes objectives, you discard it, alter it, or subject it to whatever is necessary in order to accomplish the objectives.

2. **The principle of specialization.** The work assigned to individuals should be specialized insofar

as it is consistent with effective human effort. This is the genius of the assembly line. It applies not only to assembly line situations but to managerial situations as well. The more specialized we can make the work, the more skilled the person is apt to become in that work and the more effective he is apt to be over a lengthy period. Some time ago I was consulted regarding a situation where a woman was assigned to counselling and to bookkeeping. You cannot imagine two more opposite vocations — counselling and bookkeeping. The woman was terribly frustrated because she was at an age in her life when she was affected with panic in regard to accomplishment. Usually, people at about forty tend to panic. "What have I done? What am I achieving?" Between the ages of forty and forty-five, people often make drastic changes in their vocations under the panic pressure of accomplishment. Her problem was that she was not excelling in either field. With a bit of pressure she was relieved of the bookkeeping and moved into counselling (which she preferred), and she developed an attitude which was much more wholesome. That is the kind of thing we learn from the principle of specialization.

3. **The principle of management emphasis.** When called upon to supervise two or more differing units, a manager tends to show preferential emphasis in his decisions and choices. These preferences will be determined primarily by his

previous relationships or activities. This can be good or bad, depending upon the needs of the situation.

4. **The principle of maximum span.** A manager should supervise the maximum number of people he can effectively manage. This is assuming that we view managing as a type of work to be performed and we recognize it as a legitimate assignment. The number depends upon a variety of things. Firstly, upon the capacity of the manager. Some people have a greater capacity than others. It depends secondly upon the type of work that the people who are being supervised are doing. You can obviously supervise more ditch-diggers than you can research scientists. In the third place, it depends upon geography or dispersal of the personnel. I was involved in a situation where one man was responsible for eighteen men stretched all the way across the United States and Canada. That is an impossible situation. There are not enough days in the week, there are not enough airplanes flying, and if there were the planes, he does not have the energy to supervise that many men spread over that wide an area. So it depends upon capacity; it depends upon the type of work; and it depends upon geography or the dispersal of the people that are being supervised. However, all of that being considered, the man should still supervise as many people as he can effectively manage.

5. **The principle of minimum levels.** The number of organizational levels should be kept at a mini-

mum. To proliferate the organizational levels is not necessarily to increase the effectiveness of the organization itself. We have levels going down, down, down. Minimize those levels. The more levels you multiply this way, the more difficulties you create. The reason is obvious. It takes time for information and decisions to go from the top to the bottom.

Incidentally, have you ever noticed the instinctive answer to every problem? "We are not getting the work done that we should." The first answer, the easiest answer, the spontaneous answer is, "Let us get more people." More people does not insure the accomplishment of more work. It only insures the presence of more people. Sometimes work simplification is the answer, not an increased staff. I think there is a real need for the Church around the world to re-examine whether large staffs are the cause of a low work turn-over.

6. **The principle of carry-over.** The early characteristics of organization tend to persist in later organizational forms. To put it simply, "You never outlive your past." Some of these earlier characteristics will follow you to the very end. You can make appreciable changes, but these things carry over.

Several of these principles refer to delegation.

7. **The principle of control limits.** Delegation should proceed only to the limit of effective con-

trol. Just as a person can only do so much, so he can only be accountable for so much.

8. The principle of commensurate authority. Authority should be delegated commensurate with responsibility.

9. The principle of complete accountability. The superior is always accountable for the actions of his subordinates. It is not a very pleasant position sometimes, but it is always a necessary position.

10. The principle of single reporting relationships. Each person should be accountable to only one superior.

TEN COMMANDMENTS OF GOOD ORGANIZATION

There are two kinds of efficiency. One kind is only **apparent** and is produced in organizations through the exercise of mere discipline. This is but an imitation of the second, or true, efficiency which springs, as Woodrow Wilson said, from "the spontaneous co-operation of a free people." If you are a manager, no matter how great or small your responsibility, it is your job to create and develop this voluntary co-operation among the people whom you supervise. For no matter how powerful a combination of money, machines and materials a company may have, they are dead and sterile without a team of **willing, thinking** and **articulate** people to guide them.

Here are the "Ten Commandments of Good Organization," taken from American Management Association, which I have adapted with a few word changes.

1. Definite and clear-cut responsibilities should be assigned to each person or position. We might know today what our job is, but the situation might change so that tomorrow we do not know what our job is. We need adequate supervision so that we can rediscover what our job is when we have forgotten or when it has been changed.

2. Responsibility should always be coupled with corresponding **authority.**

3. No change should be made in the scope or responsibilities of **a position** without a definite understanding to that effect on the part of all persons concerned.

4. No executive or employee, occupying a **single** position in the organization, should be subject to definite orders from more than one source. Every person should have one boss. Where it is necessary for one person to have two or three positions, there should not only be a clear understanding as to who

gives him orders with respect to which work, but also what is the time allocation for these positions. Otherwise, he is going to be torn and many people who work for him may well be frustrated because they take orders from so many people.

5. Orders should never be given to subordinates over the head of a responsible executive. The manager tells his foreman what he thinks that a certain subordinate under the latter should do; the manager does not go directly to the subordinate.

6. Criticisms of subordinates should be made privately, and in no case should a subordinate be criticized in the presence of executives or employees of equal or lower rank.

7. No dispute or difference between executive or employee as to authority or responsibilities should be considered too trivial for prompt and careful attention.

8. Promotions, wage changes, and disciplinary action should always be approved by the executive immediately superior to the one directly responsible.

9. No executive or employee should ever be required, or expected, to be at the same time an assistant to, and a critic of, another.

10.   Any executive whose work is subject to regular inspection should, whenever practicable, be given the assistance and facilities necessary to enable him to maintain an independent check of the quality of his own work. You will find he will be harder on himself than you would be on him if you make that arrangement with him. If a person is working under you, he should be given the assistance and the facilities necessary for him to evaluate how well he is doing. He should be given opportunity to report to you so that there can be not only your appraisal of his work but his appraisal of his work, both coming from the same standard.

What are the sources of authority by which a man manages? Here are four:

Firstly, the **authority of competence.** The more competent the other fellow knows you are, the more confident he will be that you know what you are talking about. And the more likely he will be to follow your orders, requests and suggestions. This does not mean that you can manage a treasurer or bookkeeper only if you yourself are an expert treasurer or bookkeeper. It means your competency as a manager in general.

Secondly, the **authority of position.** This gives you the right to tell someone else what to do. This has teeth. If you are elected chairman or director, you have to fill your position. What are the two greatest enemies of leadership? To like and to be liked. "I cannot discipline this fellow — I like him. I cannot be too hard on that man — I want him to like me." My father has worked for the International Paper Company in construction work since he was nineteen years old. He is not a Christian, but a wonderful person. Some time ago he was building a mill at Vicksburg, Mississippi, the largest paper mill in the world. I was down there to visit and he was showing me through. We were riding along in the car, and I said, "Dad, what do your men think of you?"

Dad said, "Huh, I can't talk that way to you; you're a preacher."

I said, "No, I'm really interested. What do your men think about you?"

He puffed on his cigar, looked at me and sort of grinned and said, "Well, I heard a couple of men talking in the room next to me the other day. They didn't know I was in there and one of them said, "Hendrix? Why that grey-headed old . . . .!

Dad sucked on his cigar awfully hard then, and he said, "But I don't care what they think about me. My job is to build mills and I'm building 'em and makin' money."

I thought, 'Give me that kind of courage too.' Not that ruthlessness but that kind of commitment to a purpose. If you are a "peace at any price" kind of person, you are a traitor to the cause.

Then thirdly, the **authority of your personality.** The easier it is for the other fellow to talk to you, to listen to you or to work with you, the easier he will find it to respond to your wishes. On the one hand, authoritatively fill your position; on the other hand, be as much a human being as you can possibly be. Position and personality are the two sides of the same coin.

Fourthly, the **authority of character.** This component is your credit rating with other people — that is, your reliability, your honesty, your loyalty, your sincerity, your personal morals and ethics. In the Philippines somebody said to me, "Mr. So and So? Oh, he is one of the outstanding preachers in the Republic of the Philippines, but I would not work with that man for anything. You cannot trust him. He will tell you one thing and tell somebody else on the staff just the opposite. I would not work with him." No character, no integrity, no reliability, no trustworthiness! We manage by the authority of our character — that our yea is yea and our nay is nay.

Chapter IX

DELEGATION

Delegation is one of the activities under the heading of Management Organizing.   There are three components.   But first, a definition.   What do we mean by delegation?   In a new book, Peter Drucker has three diagnostic questions for the effective managing of time.   When Drucker first got into management consulting, he realized that he had to have some way of quickly sizing up an organization, what it was doing, what it was like, and what its needs were.   He came up with three diagnostic questions:

1.   What am I doing that really does not need to be done at all by me or anyone else?

2.   Which of the activities on my time log could be handled by someone else as well if not better?

3.   What do I do that wastes the time of other people?

Drucker went on to say, amplifying on these three points, that he discovered that a well-managed plant, office, business, organization is always dull—DULL! The recurrent crisis is by far the most common symptom of poor management. I think he is right.

Delegation is learning how to identify the work that we are doing and devising methods of passing these pieces of work on to other people, but maintaining a supervisory check on these activities. In Japan one of our Japanese pastors came to me and said, "Mr. Hendrix, I would like to ask you a question." I braced myself. He said, "There is an old Japanese proverb and I want to ask you if you think this proverb is true and accurate. It goes this way: 'A wise prince or lord knows even how many ashes are in the stove in the kitchen.' Is this a good proverb?" I tried to figure out what he was getting at and answered, "No, that is not a good proverb. A wise prince or lord does not know necessarily how many ashes there are in the stove, but he knows he has someone who does know how many ashes are in the kitchen stove." The pastor smiled. I am afraid I gave him some ammunition against some of my colleagues. Not that he needed it — I think he had enough of his own.

Now, what is delegation? Many attempts have been made to define delegation. One, for example, says, "Delegation is giving others the right to make your decisions." Another says, "Delegation is to give authority to accompany responsibility." "Delegation is having other people do part of your work" is still another. I think all

of these are inadequate. I would like us to agree
on Allen's definition that, "Delegation is entrust-
ing responsibility and authority and establishing
lines of accountability."

The Need for Delegation. Why should we
consider delegation? Here are some reasons for
delegating:

1. You are not doing the big jobs that need to
be done. That is your job as the top executive.
Or someone says, "Communications have broken
down in our organization." Someone else says,
"I don't know what my job is." That is your
job, to help them find out what their job is.
Demoralization has set in. Your job is to work
on that. Now you are not doing these big jobs
that need to be done. Therefore, you should consider delegation.

2. You are missing deadlines. One day I sat
down with Clarence Jones before I made my first
trip and I said, "Clarence, you are a veteran,
travelling everywhere, teaching people and lectur-
ing on various subjects. Give me some guidelines.
Tell me what to do and what not to do as I make
this trip." He said, "Well, it is important to
work on other people's time clock. Do not take
your own American time clock."

I have tried to do this and I suppose that
deadlines are not as important in some cultures

as they are in others. It may be true in Asia; I do not know. I know, for example, that in Japan the more important a letter is, the more time you give to contemplation before you answer it. An immediate response, instead of being the epitome of efficiency, is the representation of laxity and unconcern. I know that about Japan. However, where deadlines are important, you should meet them. Sometimes you are caught in cross-cultural situations where to miss deadlines is to create demoralization in a Western staff; maybe it does it in another culture too. At any rate, if you are missing deadlines, if you are backlogged so that you cannot get things done when they are supposed to be done, you need to consider delegation.

3. You now spend time on trivial tasks that others could do. Here, we get a problem of false modesty where we say, "Well, I'm not too good. I can't do that." We come to our service for Jesus Christ, recognizing that there are some things which we will do that no one else can do or will do. But we must not let trivial tasks force us into a corner, particularly when all they do is to feed our own ego and our estimation of how humble we are.

4. You have men who, if trained, could handle the job better than you. One of our biggest problems in Christian work is our failure to properly appraise the potentialities of the people with whom we work.

5. You have an imbalance in the work load of your men. Some men are under-loaded and others are overloaded. You must help the overloaded to delegate for themselves. One of the hardest things in the world is to teach a person to look always at his work with the view, "Who can I get to do this so that I can give myself to a more important task?" We allow things that we do ourselves to become boss-imposed and system-imposed activities, instead of pushing them out and seeing that other people get them done. It is easier and we are more comfortable and more secure when we are doing it ourselves. That is reverting to operating instead of managing.

6. You have men who need new worlds to conquer. They need new spheres of responsibility.

The Ethics of Delegation. For a long time I ran into all kinds of resistance when I talked about delegation, and I could not understand it. Why do Christian workers fight the concept of delegation? Finally, one man said, "How can I give someone else the right and the authority and the assignment to do what God has called me to do?" I realized this was an ethical problem. This problem is very real and I do not minimize it. If God has called me to do something, then I cannot easily or lightly turn away from that and let somebody else take it up. But I think this ethical problem is answered completely by going back again to the three ingredients of delegation, principally emphasizing accountability. Although I have delegated a piece of work, I ultimately retain the responsibility and the accountability for its performance. Many times people have demonstrated to me their frustration because they gave somebody something to do and then, at the last minute, they discovered that it had not been done. Who is responsible? In the final analysis, those who delegated are responsible. I think this answers, then, the ethical question that comes with regard to delegation. If I give somebody else a job to do and have an understanding that they are going to do it, I cannot just turn my back and walk away from it. I am still responsible, and if it does not get done I have to answer for it. Mr. Harry Truman in his Presidential office used to have a sign worth remembering, "The buck stops here." Every manager ought to have that mentality. I am responsible and from this office there is no passing the buck! If the person did not do it, it is my fault.

Henry Brandt says, "People do what we **inspect** not what we **expect**." And it simply means that you have to solemnly and relentlessly inspect and establish lines for accountability. You have to accept that the best man you have may not be able to follow through on a given assignment unless you continually supervise and check back and give concern, help and direction. To me this answers the ethical question.

We are always in a state of conflict concerning what we would like to do and what we are gifted to do. People who have been in the ministry fifty years are still struggling with it. I do not have an easy answer, but I have developed some answers that satisfy me. I have decided never to desire to do anything that requires gifts my brethren do not recognize in me. I am not an individualist; I am a member of the body, a part of the organization. I will continually accept that I tend to have exaggerated notions of my abilities.

There are some barriers to delegation. Why is it that delegation is so difficult? Here are some reasons for resistance to delegation:

1. There is a reluctance to admit limitation or the fear of competition. That is very real. There are always people who are willing to take real responsibility for some segment of the work if the other person is willing to let go. The biggest problem is getting the person at the top to let go. (II Tim. 2:2 "And the things thou hast heard of me among many witnesses, the same commit thou to faithful men who shall be able to teach others also.")

2. Tradition, desire for prestige, desire to retain control.

3. Lack of confidence in your men. The more insecure we are, the more we tend to look with disdain upon the capacity of the people around us because, we think, that makes us look better or bigger. Why is this? I am not sure that I know

the reason, but we ought to be **the** people of all people who are poised and confident.   Is it that we are so possessive of our positions and so defensive of our organizations and have such a minimum of goal commitment?

4.   You doubt your ability to train someone else to do it your way.   Many times our appraisal is on the basis of "how" something is done, not "whether" it is done.

5.   Expense in time and training, mistakes, and a lack of uniformity enter in too.   Great things have not been done by perfectionists but by activists.   Study history with that in view.   Possibly the exceptions would be the scientists, the researchers, the musician, or the artist.   As far as human enterprise is concerned, it has been the activists.

6.   Ignorance.   Some of us have never seen it done properly.

Let us summarize.   We have said that all of the reasons for a man resisting delegation are within him, not outside him.   All the reasons for resisting delegation are emotional.   It is something within him that blocks him, not something from without.   The barrier, then, is EMOTIONAL.

CHAPTER X

JOB DESCRIPTIONS

The subject of **Job Description** relates dynamically and vitally to the whole PLOC concept. Let us look again at the outline and relate the subject of Job Descriptions to it. There are two places where job descriptions might be considered. I believe Louis Allen inserts job descriptions into the subject of establishing objectives. Job descriptions can be there or under the subject of delegating. I feel it belongs under objectives because normally delegating has to do with situations that are not covered in a formal job description. Here we take objectives as referring not only to corporate and departmental, but also to individual responsibilities.

The extent to which you grasp this may determine largely the relevance of this book to your future. I hope you will see how this subject can relate to your own situation. It is my absolute conviction that all of us in Christian work should have job descriptions and those job descriptions should be living, dynamic things like the organizing structure. A job description, if it has not been reviewed with the people concerned, the boss and the subordinate, at least once a year, up-dated, retyped and re-issued, is antiquated. It may be doing more harm than good.

Job descriptions are very important. A job description helps us know what our tasks are and why we are in the organization. A job description helps our boss to know what we are doing. It helps us to know what he expects of us, and it lets people around us know what we are doing. Likewise we know why their jobs exist. Very few people in industry have job descriptions. Many businesses do not have job descriptions. If they do, often they are unrelated, irrelevant, out of date and quite a caricature — not really representative of what the person is doing — in which case it is tragic.

The more technical and specific and routine the function, the easier it is to write the job description but the less the description is needed. The more innovative, creative, imaginative the job, the greater the need for the job description but the more difficult to write. For example, a person doing linguistic work is assigned to a tribe to reduce a language to writing. It is easy, relatively speaking, to write that man's job description. But if you have a job assigned to a church planter that is very difficult to write, but this man needs it more than the linguist. The more technical the work, the easier it is to write the job description. Take a situation in the MAF (Missionary Aviation Fellowship). It will be a great deal easier to write the job description of a man whose job it is to repair engines than it is to write the job description for the man who is the Field Director. The more managerial the job, the more difficult to write the description. But the more managerial the function, the more important it is to write the job description.

Job descriptions show us what we are supposed to do and show our boss what we are doing. Even if you are in a voluntary situation where you are not paid at all, job descriptions are still very important. Some of the most effective churches I know in America have job descriptions for their deacons and their Sunday School superintendents and their Sunday School teachers. And you might think that people stand off and say, "Oh, I don't want a job description. I'm just serving the Lord." But these people say, "I'm glad to know what is expected of me." It puts teeth into our organizational structure, and it gives clarity and clear, sharp lines to relationships. More than any other singular mechanical device, job descriptions give us a goal-orientation. When you start writing down the end result for which a job exists, you had better come with a goal-orientation or find out how to live with a fellow who is pretending and bluffing his way through. Here you can develop, and will develop, a goal-orientation. Job descriptions should be specific, definite, and measurable. They should have teeth; they should be binding; they should be clear.

In a seminar some time ago I gave a lecture on job descriptions and then assigned the people to write down their own job description. Here is a job description that I received. They followed my suggested format — the job summary, the job duties, the organizational relationships, the qualifications and the development. What do you think of this? "JOB SUMMARY — To live in a certain named village in such a spiritual, Christ-honouring way as to turn residents of this village from darkness to light. JOB DUTIES — 1) To maintain a constant fellowship with God, so as to live a sinless, perfect example in dependence upon the Holy Spirit. 2) Be ready at all times to give a reason for the hope that is in you. 3) Give unselfishly of your time and talents to any worthy cause within the village which might result in winning some. 4) Write a report at least once a month. ORGANIZATIONAL RELATIONSHIPS — Responsible to God alone — He who will judge the quick and the dead. Responsible for — those in the village whom God has predestinated to enter into His glorious fellowship. QUALIFICATIONS — should be a spiritually-minded person of highest integrity; if possible, should have completed Bible School. TRAINING AND DEVELOPMENT — should be skilled in using the Word of God for the winning of precious souls."

In the light of what I said job description ought to be, this is ambigous and has no measurement, but it sounds so pretty! Do you know what good this will do? It will just inflate the man's already overinflated spiritual ego.

The kind of a job description format you use is unimportant. If you go to the library and check a hundred books on management in which the subject of job descriptions is dealt with, you will find a hundred suggestions or formats. For example, there was an article recently on how to write a job description for a pastor. The format was altogether different, but in the end it accomplished the same thing. Generally, they all come out at the same place, though the building of them is entirely different.

Firstly, at the beginning of your job description you need a Job Title. The Job Title should be as descriptive as possible of the work that is performed. Where you are involved with precedent and tradition and cannot make changes, use whatever terms the situation dictates. The title should describe as nearly as possible the work that is being filled or accomplished by this position. Then, you need the name of the individual involved. There are only two places where the individual himself is brought into play — at the top of the sheet and in the last point, **TRAINING AND DEVELOPMENT.**

The other sections of this job description could apply to any individual. Next, write the date. This is important because once twelve months have elapsed, it is out of date! There are very few job descriptions that can go on for more than a year without alterations, because the environment changes, the capacities of the individual change and the needs of the office change. The person managing has to keep this constantly in review. In more intricate, complex situations you may want to indicate the department or the division. For example, a person may be in the Evangelism Department, the Church-Planting Department, or the Radio Department of a mission, or he may be in the Laboratory Department of a hospital. This simply further breaks down and pinpoints where this man fits in the organization. Adapt these things any way you see fit to meet the demands of your organization.

The job description consists of five parts:

1. **THE JOB SUMMARY.** This is the most difficult to write. The Job Summary reflects the position of the organizational chart. The Job Summary is built into that total pyramid (see page 71). There should be a short-range and a long-range pyramid. The Job Summary places a person into the pyramid wherever he belongs, and is aimed at accomplishing the goal of the total organization. The Job Summary puts in words the end result this position exists to accomplish. Particularly when you ask someone for whom you are responsible to begin working on their own job description, you are going to find that sometimes they do not know why they are

there. This has to do with purpose, with objectives, with goals, with targets. Not only this but you are going to discover that you have positions for which there is no valid reason. That is a fact. If you take this matter seriously, you will find that there are people on the payroll involved in the activities who have no definitive, specific purpose for their operation. The Job Summary, the end result the job exists to accomplish, is the most difficult thing to write in all of the job description. It must be measurable, definitive and specific.

2. **THE JOB DUTIES.** These are the activities necessary for the accomplishment of the above-mentioned end result. This is the easiest thing to write, particularly if you just write down what the person is presently doing. If that is all you do, you have not written a job description. You have only given the man a piece of paper to justify the continuation of his activities, and that may be bad. Do not come to **DUTIES** until you have settled the end result before the Lord.

Once this is settled, you will want to list the activities that are necessary for the accomplishment of the above-mentioned position. Here you begin to draw some very distinct lines between the various positions that exist in your organization, and begin to eliminate overlap. This can help the function of an organization where a man, while he retains an extremely sensitive team-conciousness and concept, recognizes "I'm praying for this man over here who is doing so and so, but that is his job and this is mine." And he is concerned and he is involved. He is available to help if he is needed, but that is not his job and he does not meddle or interfere. Even though he is the manager he is not going to make another man's decision. He has his own work to do.

3. **ORGANIZATIONAL RELATIONSHIPS.** Here we are back to the organizational chart. Organizational relationships extend in four directions: up, down, and sideways in both directions. This should show a man exactly what his relationship is to his superior, exactly what his relationship is to his subordinate and what his relationship is to people on either side of him. This works in a church where a Sunday School department leader realizes "I take my orders with respect to the operation of this Sunday School from Mr. So and So. I am responsible to oversee these people. I know there is another department functioning over here and this man has the same kind of authority and responsibility that I have." You do not have to pay a man's salary in order to do this. It works beautifully in a voluntary situation like a Sunday School or in a more complex situation like General Motors. The two key words are TO and FOR. Responsible to — that shows superiors; responsible for — that designates subordinates. It is important to note the difference between "staff" and "line" relationships. A staff relationship means service, information, consultation and advice. This person or committee has

no authority. He does not issue any orders. In the chart, the broken line indicates a "staff" relationship over against a "line" relationship. In other words, this man or group serves in an advisory capacity rather than in an authoritative and decision-making role.

4. QUALIFICATIONS. These are for the performance of this work. This is what the person should **ideally** be and know in order to most effectively accomplish the Job Summary. If you omit the individual's name then you can write job descriptions for functions you eventually want accomplished in your organization for which you neither have men nor money now. This helps tremendously. It is not a matter of who is available; it is a matter of "here is what we want done. Where is the person, anywhere in the world, that can best do it?" That makes a difference in filling positions in your church. Here is what we are trying to accomplish by this church and what needs to be done in this position. Here are the qualifications. Where is the man? You set your standard high. It is realistic.

At this point you personalize the job description under the heading of

5. TRAINING AND DEVELOPMENT. In other words, this man does not ever measure up fully to these qualifications. He needs self-development to better qualify. I know I am on thin ice. We are not supposed to develop self, but to

reckon self dead. I realize that, but we are talking about skills, not morals, not spirituality. If we agree on this, then we can go on and intelligently use some terms like self-development. What is wrong with a man going to school and learning something in order to better do the job that he recognizes God has called him to do? That is self-development. Is that evil? If the key to training and development is that it must be specific, then training and development must project itself for no more than twelve months.

In other words, here is a man. This man does not quite measure up. No man does. If he does, revise your qualifications and get them up higher. What training and development can we give to this man in order to better qualify him? You do not unilaterally determine this and hand it to him on a slip of paper as you go past him one morning. This is a mutually-agreed thing. He will be harder on himself than you would be if you let him be. Do not think of training and development as just going to school. You can learn without going to a university. There are other places to develop your skills. For example, one of our men needed development in a certain area. We inquired around and did some research and found, as far as we were able to determine, the one man in America that knew more about this subject than any other man. We wrote to him and said, "If we send our man out, can he sit at your elbow for a couple of weeks and just watch what you do?" That is training and development.

Training and development says, "Mr. A. is going to California. He is going to be an understudy with Mr. B. from October 1 to October 15. It will cost us 'X' number of dollars." That is training and development. It may include formal situations. Training and development does not necessarily mean going back to seminary. That is not the kind of training and development most of us need. Rather, we need a Dale Carnegie course, or a speed-reading course, or a course in public relations, or a course in some skill that relates to the type of work that we are doing. This training and development is specific. It is dated. It is to compensate for the man's inadequacies as they are spelled out in this list of qualifications. I know this is work, but it will transform any operation you are in — if you will do it.

Chapter XI

MANAGEMENT LEADING PRINCIPLES

Under the subject of management-leading comes decision-making. Leading is the work in which we engage to inspire and, where necessary, impel people to take action. There are eleven management-leading principles according to Louis Allen, which cover all the activities or components of management-leading. Some of them apply to decision-making because that is one of the components of leading. Some apply to communications. Some apply to motivation and some to selecting and developing people.

Here we take the subject of decision-making.

A. DECISION-MAKING

Someone described a manager as a man who makes decisions. Sometimes he makes the right ones, but he always makes them. We insist upon infallibility in decision-making for ourselves and for people who work with us, but we will not tolerate or allow weakness, or mistakes, particularly in other people. We are much more tolerant of ourselves than we are of the person who is working with us or under our supervision. If you are in a place of leadership you have to make decisions. Hesitancy on your part in deciding will breed deep demoralization and frustration in your ranks. The longer it takes a man to make a decision in your organization, the more encumbered you are and the more you are saying to that man, "Your time and activities are of minimal importance." Hesitancy in decision-making, or proliferation, or encumbrance of structure for the purpose of decision breeds demoralization and frustration. This says to a man, "What you are doing is not important enough for a quick decision."

Why do we have such difficulties in making decisions? One reason is the control-orientation organization. We would prefer to have everyone involved in the decision than to having the decision made effectively and accomplishing our goal. This is a part of our degeneracy. To make decisions involves risk. Many people hedge on decision-making and would prefer to do anything rather than to decide.

There are three principles which apply to decision-making:

First, a logical decision can be reached only if the problem is first defined. There is a vast difference between problem-identification and problem-solving or decision-making. Problem-solving, comparatively speaking, is easy. Problem-identification is extremely difficult. Most of us do not take time to identify problems. We plunge in to solve them. Problems, because they are related to human beings, take on the manifestation of the facade — one of the chief characteristics of the human being. When you sit down with an individual and say, "How are you?" he will seldom tell you right off how he really is. A person comes to you for counselling. "Tell me what your problem is" you begin. He will seldom say at first what his real problem is. He will throw up first the facade. We are creatures of the facade and because problems are so intimately entwined with human beings, we tend to manifest a false front. When we begin approaching problems and dealing with them, if we are not careful we merely deal with the symptoms and not with the real problem. We must persevere to adequately define the problem.

Secondly, the principle of adequate evidence teaches us that a logical decision must be valid in terms of the evidence upon which it is based. Our problem in Christ's work is our utter subjectivity. Our subjectivity builds a high protective wall around us so that everything about us is immune to the criticism of our fellowmen because we have prayed about it or the Lord has led us. I am not speaking lightly about prayer or of divine guidance. But if he is not very careful, these things can be protective walls around an individual who is basically evasive.

122 MANAGEMENT/CHRISTIAN WORKER

Thirdly, the principle of identity or scope. This principle teaches us that facts may appear to differ, depending upon the point of view and the point in time from which they are observed. In other words, the decisions we make are valid or invalid depending upon how and when we look at them. This is why decisions made today look so stupid tomorrow.

These three principles have to do with decision-making. Next, let us consider the logical thinking process. It consists of a series of questions. I do not expect that you are going to take these questions and apply them to every decision. But if you can apply them to a major decision soon it can help you immeasurably. It will form a pattern in your subconscious mind in adapting to various types of problem situations. The questions in the logical thinking process, in sequence order, are as follows:

1. **What Is The Apparent Problem?**

2. **What Are The Facts?** Because some of us are theologically-oriented and think we have a pipeline to omniscience, we cannot afford to be bothered with the assimilation of facts. After all, we have a revelation! Somebody said, "Are you gathering facts or merely re-arranging prejudices?" Here you need to get the situation factor, the people factor, the place factor, the time factor, the causative factor, and then assimilate all the facts you can.

3. **What Is The Real Problem?** Do not ask this question until you have adequately dealt with the two previous ones! Remember the facade!

4. **What Are The Possible Solutions?** Generally, the possible solutions that emerge spontaneously to your mind will be extremes. That is the way we solve problems instinctively, intuitively, natively. We just get hold of the pendulum and swing as hard as we can from one extreme to the other. These extreme solutions may need to be considered, but do not settle for two alternative and diametrically opposed solutions. There is always a third solution. It will seldom manifest itself easily, but do not stop until you find a third solution to the problem. When you find the third, you will often find that it will open up a whole new vista with a fourth, fifth and sixth solution.

5. **What Course Of Action Shall We Follow?**

Alternatively, here are four questions which outline the total analysis required by any decision large or small:

1. Do I really understand the problem?

2. What am I trying to get done?

3. Is this the way to do it?

4. What will go wrong when I put this decision into action?

You are not going to solve one problem without creating some others. Hopefully you will create some lesser problems. Nevertheless, in most problem solving there are some negative consequences. Anticipate them. What is going to go wrong when I put this decision into effect?

B. COMMUNICATIONS

David Sarnoff of RCA said, "The power to communicate is the power to lead." I do not think anyone who has been involved in a managerial position will doubt this assertion.

Following Louis A. Allen's management-leading principles, we note that there are three which apply to communication:

1. The principle of line loss. The effectiveness of communication tends to vary inversely with its extension. Suppose I took fifteen men, lined them up around the room, and then read in the ear of one man just a headline from the morning paper. By the time that headline was transmitted verbally from man to man around the room, there would be little or no resemblance with what came from man fifteen as compared with what went into man one! The effectiveness of communication tends to vary inversely with its extension. The more levels it has to go

through, the more minds and tongues that filter it, the more distorted it becomes. There is no sense in getting angry about this and there is no sense in blaming people when something is repeated back to you, fifth or sixth hand, and you are quoted incorrectly.

2. The principle of emotional appeal. Appeals to emotions are communicated more readily than appeals to reason. If you preachers could get hold of this it could revolutionize your preaching. We are so logical. We follow such strict forms of apologetics and we have everything unanswerably set forth. The only problem is that no one hears it. It does not grip anyone. Study the great teachers and preachers of history and you will find that they have found emotional pegs upon which to hang their thoughts.

3. The principle of application. The more a communication is used and applied, the better it will be understood and remembered. Some of us do a lot of talking but not much teaching — a lot of preaching but not much communicating. Why? Because maybe we only say it once or twice, or a dozen times, and that is not enough. Sometimes a thing has to be said over and over and over again.

What is communication? I want to give you a definition from the Word of God. In this passage there is one word which, more than any other word, tells us what communication is.

I Cor. 14: 7-9 "And even things without life giving sound, whether pipe or harp, except they give a distinction in the sounds, how shall it be known what is piped or harped? For if the trumpet give an uncertain sound, who shall prepare himself for battle? So, likewise, except ye utter by the tongue words easy to be understood, how shall it be known what is spoken? For ye shall speak into the air." (A. V.) It is the word, "understood." Communication is the work we do to secure **understanding** between ourselves and another human being.

The big problem in communication is words — because words tend to obscure meaning and not clarify meaning. According to the Oxford English Dictionary, the five hundred most-used words in the English language have an average of twenty-three meanings each. The word "round" has seventy distinctly different meanings. This is not the only problem we face. We have a vocabulary that would impress the dictionary! Another problem we have is that words are symbols only. Words represent ideas; they are not ideas themselves. Words are symbols, not things.

The problem that we are confronted with is that we have a man with an idea. He wants to communicate that idea to another person. How is he going to transmit an idea from his brain to the other person's brain? It can be a theological idea, a mechanical idea, a philosophical idea, etc. Obviously, his first recourse is going to be words.

They may be written or spoken, softly or loudly. Words are the main instrument at his disposal to communicate or transmit this idea from his mind to another human being's mind. The whole process of transmitting the idea by words to another is beclouded by many issues and we want to see them as we go along. Dr. Hendricks of Dallas describes the difficulty in conveying not just a concept but a "concept feeling." His point is that we do not convey concepts only. That is impossible. We convey "concept feelings." The two are inseparable. It is not just a cold idea. It is an idea that is coupled with feeling. Sometimes it is an intense feeling; sometimes not so intense; sometimes a negative feeling; sometimes a feeling of hate or love. Still there is a feeling to some degree connected with every concept.

Why do we get into such trouble when it comes to communication? There are four points or stages in the process of communication. We begin with the all-important process of **asking.** We do not adequately communicate with another until we have asked questions. I must know the person's mind in some degree before I communicate with him. The complexity and the intricacies of the message determine how much I must know about that person's mind. For example, if I want to say, "Shut the door," I do not have to know a great deal about the person or his thinking processes in order to communicate that feeling concept. But let us say I want to communicate a theological or philosophical idea to this fellow. Where he was born, how he was brought up, what his family situation was like, where he went to school, what books he has read in the last five years — a thousand things can enter in here.

How do I discover what another human being is like? By looking at the colour of his skin? By looking at the colour of his eyes? By looking at whether he is fat or skinny? NO! These are externals. They have nothing to do with what is inside the man. There is one way you get to the man on the inside and that is to ask questions. Some of us do not communicate simply because we either do not have the time to ask questions or we do not know how to ask questions.

There are three basic types of questions:

First, there is the informational type of questions. These have to do with statistics and facts. Questions like: How many? Who? How much? Where? When? Informational questions are inoffensive questions. You can always say to a person, "Where do you work?" "How many people are involved?" without getting a reaction.

Secondly, there is the ideational type of questions. This is where you ask the person what he thinks or what he suggests or what he feels. Like informational questions, ideational questions are also safe. You will not create trouble or give offense when you are asking a subordinate ideational questions.

The third type of questions is different. This is the evaluation question and is always dangerous. This is where you ask a man to evaluate his work, his ideas, his concepts, or anything with which he is associated or involved. These kinds of questions are strategic questions and they tend to become tremendously subjective questions. If you ask evaluative questions of an individual before you have asked ideational or informational questions you may alienate him. We are what we are and it is a proven fact that we are more willing to give evaluative information after we have had an opportunity to express our ideas and to give information, particularly information which we feel the other person may not have about us or our work. We need to ask questions that fit the need.

Let me show some differences. Ask "open questions" not "closed questions." Open questions invite the other person to express freely what he feels. They never make him feel that he is boxed in. Here is an example of an open question: "Tell me, Joe, how does this problem look to you?" The person can go on from that to express what he really feels. A closed question is a kind of question that forces the other person to a point of view other than his own. It is a kind of question that makes him feel like he has to conform to what we already think. Here is an example of a closed question: "Now, Joe, if you were convinced that taking this action is morally wrong, you wouldn't be for it would you?" What can he say? You have closed him out. He only has one answer.

Ask leading questions, not loaded ones! Leading questions give direction to the reply but they are not restrictive to any one way. Here is an example of a leading question: "How did you go about working out your solution to the problem, Joe?" But a loaded question puts the respondent in a difficult position — whatever his answer may be. An example of a loaded question is: "What made you think that your solution to the problem was the right one?" You have made this fellow defensive. Defensiveness is one of the most detrimental and constantly recurring attitudes in Christian work. Not hatred. Not animosity. Not bitterness. I see these things occasionally, but the most universally detrimental emotion and attitude I find in Christian work is defensiveness. I wonder sometimes if we do not make people defensive.

Ask cool questions and not heated ones. The cool question appeals to reason and involves the emotion as little as possible. A question, on the other hand, reflects the feeling of the questioner and incites the feelings of the respondent. Here is the cool question: "Now what would you say the first step towards a solution should be, Joe?" And the heated question: "We've already been round and round on that one, so what do you think we should do?" The person has to produce there or be embarrassed.

The second step in the communication process is **telling** — articulating — putting in words the message you have to get across. Unfortunately, we often plunge into telling before we have done any asking. How do we go about telling? I am going to digress considerably from purely managerial communication situations to talk about communications in general because most of you are preachers and teachers. At least we are involved to some degree in preaching and teaching. How do we communicate our message from our minds to the minds of a group of people? Here are four steps to good telling:

The first step is — Get an audience. Attract the attention! Here is a brain that is in absolute neutral, an emotion that is just disengaged, an anatomy in which there presently is functioning no capacity for receiving a communication. Now the person may be in church or in Sunday School or in a seminar, but there he sits — neutral! **Get an audience!** It is not easy.

There was a farmer who sold a mule to another person down the road. He explained carefully to the purchaser,

"This old mule is a good old mule but you must be gentle with him, ever so gentle."

The next day about ten o'clock, the purchaser appeared at the door of the seller, most irate, demanding his money back. The seller said,

"What's wrong?"

"That mule is sitting in the middle of the barnyard and will not move. I have been ever so gentle all morning with him and there he sits."

"Oh," the seller said, "Let me help you."

So they went down to the purchaser's barnyard and there sat the mule. He looked around the barnyard. He got a big stick and walked over to him and hit him as hard as he could right on the head. The old mule staggered around and got up on his feet. The man said,

"But I thought you said you had to be gentle."

"You do, but first you have to get his attention!"

We often talk without getting anyone's attention.

Step two in good telling is. **Build a bridge.** Build a bridge from what you say to what he is interested in. I like young people.   I would rather smell perfume than liniment! I like young people — their imagination, their drive, their colour, the sparkle in their eyes. Frankly, I do not think that all young people have deteriorated. The one complaint I hear most frequently from young people about preaching in America is, "Well, what's all that got to do with where I am? Why bring that up? We hear these learned dissertations on this subject and that, but they are wide off the mark. They make no point of contact with us." We cannot get through to them until we learn to build a bridge from where we are to where they are.

Number three: **Illustrate!** You may have heard Dr. Donald Grey Barnhouse preach. In my estimation, Dr. Barnhouse was one of the greatest illustrators of our day. I would recommend that you read his sermons and books. The man was a masterful illustrator. Eerdman's have published a book entitled, LET ME ILLUSTRATE by Barnhouse.   Study the illustrations of the New Testament. You will find that in most instances Bible illustrations use things that people handle and with which they are thoroughly conversant and familiar.

Point number four in good telling is: **Ask for action.** It was Sangster in his book, THE CRAFT OF THE SERMON, who said that the whole point of a sermon is to ask for action. We might say this about almost any communication. There is a sense in which the whole point of a communication is to ask for action.

I want to review for you in a few sentences a book that made a very great impression on me. The John Knox Press in Richmond, Virginia, U.S.A. have published a book entitled WORDS ON TARGET by Sue Nichols, a Presbyterian journalist.   She introduces her book by emphasizing the responsibility that rests upon the Christian communicator.   She begins by showing what a difference it makes whether we are trying to communicate in the 19th century or the 20th century. There are several examples given of 19th century plays — melodramas — which are staged in all seriousness. When these things were put on originally they were moving, forceful experiences, evoking tears from participating audiences. When they were put on in the 20th century with equal seriousness, do you know what reaction they evoked? Laughter! Hilarity! Not a tear anywhere! Why? The 19th century was different from the 20th century. You'd think that we would know this but we do not.

She goes on and says that there are three essential ingredients in communication. These are:

1. We must communicate **economically.** There must be economy in our communication. Economy in communication means communicating without any unnecessary words. Play back one of your sermons sometime. Listen to the superfluous words. What do they do? They obstruct communication.

2. We must communicate with words of **energy,** words of force. How long has it been since you added a new word to your vocabulary? This is one thing you can do. All of you probably have access to the READER'S DIGEST. Work those little vocabulary builders. Make it a point to learn at least one new word every week and make sure they are easy words. Make sure

they are words that will carry an impact. Some of you may have heard Dr. R.G. Lee, one of the greatest preachers of our day, an orator par excellence. Somebody was complimenting Lee one day on a sermon.

They said, "Dr. Lee, the thing that is so unforgettable is your choice of words."

He said, "Oh, don't talk to me about words. I struggle with words."

We do not take very seriously our vocabulary. Work on it. Discover words of energy to convey to your men.

3. We must communicate by **subtlety.** Her point is that we must be listeners, the readers' eyes and ears, but we dare not be his brain or his will. Listening is the third stage in the process of communication. We have tried to learn how to do about everything but listen. Andrew Carnegie said, "Any fool can speak with a glib tongue. Send me a man who listens." A lot of us do not communicate because we do not listen. How many times people have said about another person, "I cannot get his ear." That is a sad commentary. Learn how to listen.

In the process of communication the final stage is **understanding,** i.e. where two human beings understand one another. Notice that communication is not agreement, but it is understanding. There is a lot more misunderstanding than there is disagreement among God's people.

Let me clarify the difference between **formal** and **informal** communication. By formal communication we mean those words or letters by which we endeavour to formulate or convey a concept feeling from ourselves to another person. But this is not the only way we communicate. We communicate not only by what we say but also by how we say it, by our posture, our facial expressions, by the way we dress. Everything about us communicates! When a person drums his fingers on the table or desk, what does this say? It says volumes. "I'm bored and you are not important, so hurry up." It makes a difference how we carry ourselves, whether our shoulders are back. Do we not communicate by a positive attitude as over against a negative attitude? Do we not communicate by a spring in our step rather than a slouch in our walk? Everything about us communicates. This is why we need to consider everything that we are in our communication, the way we dress, the way we live, the way we express ourselves. Everything about us communicates. This is informal communication.

What are the barriers to communication? Where do we get into trouble? What causes our problems? Undoubtedly the biggest problem is our mistaking the medium for the process. Let me illustrate. I was conducting some meetings, in a church in Michigan, U.S.A. After one of the meetings, a group of us were standing around in the basement of the church having some coffee. The pastor's wife entered the room and she was what Dr. Howard Hendricks would call a "female dreadnaught." She steamed up to where I was, her eyes flaming with indignation. I stood there wondering whether to speak or run. After some minutes, I said, "Hello," but she just puffed and steamed. Finally I said, "Is something wrong?" Well, that was pushing her button, i.e., spurring her to action.

She said, "Those crazy women!"

I said, "Which women?"

She replied, "Those dumb women in our church."

I said, "Tell me about it."

Well did she ever tell me!!! Her whole point was "I told these people! I TOLD THESE WOMEN!" And I could not say it to her, but I thought to myself, "Yes, she told them, but that is not important. The important thing is, **did they hear her?**" It is an amazing thing. I can stand, or you can stand, in the presence of another person and tell and tell and tell and tell and tell! "Nobody ever told me." It happens every day of the week to every one of us. My seventeen year old son came out the other day with something that he had discovered. I have been telling him this for seventeen years. He never heard it, but he heard someone else say it and it registered. What was my reaction? "Well, that's great! A great discovery, Dave! I'm happy for you. Terrific!" I'm not going to tell him, "Why, I told you that!" What difference does it make? We have an exaggerated concept of the significance of what we have to say. The other fellow does not care what we have to say. When you mistake the medium for the process you have not communicated. You may have told until you were hoarse. Communication is not telling. Communication is asking, telling, listening, and understanding. It is nothing less than that. Communication is not writing a memo, for that does not ensure understanding.

The other thing is the failure to consider emotional blocks in communication. The fact, whether we like it or not, is that we are dealing with emotional creatures. You have something to tell someone. He may be inwardly distraught about things that he cannot divulge to you or anyone else. He is not going to hear what you say because he is preoccupied with his own distraction. He may be ill. Maybe he is not in pain enough that it warrants going to bed, but when a man is in pain he is preoccupied with that pain and he does not hear everything that goes on around him. Maybe he is distressed about one of his children. Or maybe something, in all innocence, was said two hours earlier which hurt that man. You may preach that self and feelings should not be felt. There is an element of truth in this, but we must remember that we are human beings.

Are we communicating with people who are human beings? The Lord Jesus understood people, their feelings, their needs and He was sympathetic with them. He knew how to say the precisely right word to an adulteress. He knew exactly how to tenderly deal with those obstinate, impenetrable minds of the disciples. Read THE TRAINING OF THE TWELVE, by A. B. Bruce. See the marvelous empathy the Lord Jesus had for those men in their obstinacy, in their darkness — the amazing ability of projecting His personality into the disciples and so fully understanding them. The Lord had this empathy for all whom He met. When he raised Jairus' daughter from the dead, the first thing He said was, "Give her something to eat." We would have been interested about getting a tract written, but not the Lord Jesus. "Give her something to eat."

CHAPTER XII

MANAGEMENT CONTROL

Management Controlling Principles: Louis Allen's definition of management controlling is: "the work we engage in to check work in progress and complete it." This is one aspect of Christian work that perplexes me greatly. How have we come to assume, or infer, that we can be thrown in together as a group of individuals with the view of accomplishing common goals without someone assuming the responsibility for checking and coordinating the work in progress? In our types of organization we come up with a whole series of people (it can be fifty or one hundred and twenty-five), allegedly banded together and moving toward an objective like the evangelization of a country and the planting of the church in that country. Yet, in the final outworking of the thing, instead of moving in union and harmony, the tendency (because of, I think, the theological emphasis in Protestantism) is for each man to follow the path of his own inclination. Dedicated men go in all kinds of directions with goals that may be similar but are seldom coordinated. The point of management controlling is, once the goal has been identified, once the relationships have been determined, once the work has been assigned, once the decision-making power or authority has been clearly defined, controlling says, "We are going to ensure that we all go in this one direction." Do not allow yourself to think thoughts like this, "Well, it has not been done in this way in faith missions heretofore." No one is more aware of this than I am and yet I still presume to emphasize that the subject is valid. Do not assume that our organization is so different, everyone is just simply too individualistic. We **can** expect to achieve this kind of union towards our objective. It **can** be done.

Management control can be implemented in order that we can together accomplish this goal with everyone moving towards it. What do we have in missions and in churches, generally? We have a man at the top, frequently insecure and very unsure of what he is supposed to do. Often he is so totally oblivious of the value of management controlling, that he simply assumes or hopes that everyone will move toward the objective when he exerts a little pressure and influence and commits the work to God in prayer. Frequently, when objectives are not being accomplished, and while there is work being done and signs of activity evident, those in positions of leadership do not take any action. But as the situation deteriorates and worsens, men in leadership begin to be concerned. They begin to pray. They could go further and implement management control. An individual responsible for the group should begin to check the work in progress against the performance standards that have been established. I think we harm our mission workers; in deference to their demands to be individualists, we let them wander all over the place without reining them in tight and controlling their activities and saying, "Here is the direction we are going. We are trying to accomplish this. Here is your role. Now play that role." We all have come into the Lord's work because of the strong goal-orientation. This individualism emerges after we are in the group, not before. It is not the product of what we were before we got into the group. We came into the group because we wanted to move in union with other men toward the accomplishment of the goal. What is the problem? The problem is the leadership. There has not been a man at the top who is so goal-oriented that he gives the order and says, "We are going to do this. Here is your role." The man may make mistakes. He may have to go back and say, "Excuse me, Joe, we blundered on that project. I am awfully sorry. Now let us try again and go towards this goal" But this does not happen. I am absolutely appalled and I cannot understand the lack of direction that exists in societies today. Some of you may come from highly goal-oriented missions where there is adequate supervisory pressure at the top to move people in unison, but generally speaking this is not so.

We must always respect people as human beings, not pieces of machinery, not just some inanimate object that you place in some place and say, "Do this," and he does it. No, these are human beings, but they are human beings who want to accomplish a goal.

Occasionally you will meet a Christian worker who does not want to accomplish anything. Sometimes you will have to remove him from the pursuit of this goal and send him home. If one of these men embezzled $60,000, you would cane him. If he becomes involved in heresy, you ship him off. But he can wander around ineffectively on the field, and we do not do anything about it. I want to insist that it is not his fault. It is Mr. A's fault, the man at the top; or maybe we should say, it is the men at the top.

So many things begin to merge here and come to the fore: the goal-orientation, organization, the job description, communications, establishing and maintaining inter-human relationships, the authority by which we manage, etc. However, the persons who are wandering around all over the place are not to blame themselves. Let us remember that the followers of the Lord Jesus Christ are called "sheep" and the continuing need for any sheep is a shepherd. We recognize this spiritually and we appoint undershepherds but this is equally important in the practical outworkings of our lives. Why is there this dichotomy between the practical and the spiritual? Why is it that people look at this subject and say, "Oh, well, this is not spiritual." I beg to differ. Is

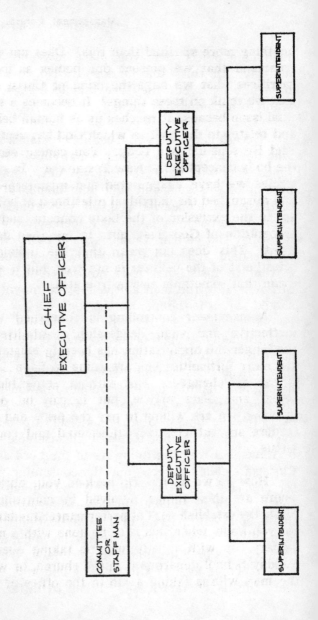

ORGANIZATIONAL CHART

SEE PAGES 74, 115-116

CHIEF EXECUTIVE OFFICER

COMMITTEE OR STAFF MAN

DEPUTY EXECUTIVE OFFICER

DEPUTY EXECUTIVE OFFICER

SUPERINTENDENT

SUPERINTENDENT

SUPERINTENDENT

SUPERINTENDENT

anything more spiritual than this? Does not God command that we present our bodies as living sacrifices, that we have the mind of Christ and that we think on these things? It becomes a spiritual issue because it touches us as human beings and relates to the goal to which God has sent us. And He sent us as a body. You cannot escape the body concept in the New Testament. In some circles we have exaggerated and misinterpreted and misapplied the individual priesthood of believers to the exclusion of the body concept, and the recognition of God-given gifts to our own detriment. This does not mean that the individual priesthood of the believer is not true, but it does mean that something else is true also.

Management controlling is concerned with ineffective and vague leadership. Admittedly, the longer the organization has been in existence, the more difficulties you are going to have. But it can be changed! Not without some blood, sweat and tears maybe, but it can be done provided we are willing to pay the price and the leaders are sufficiently goal-oriented and courageous.

How do we do it? Go back to your outline. There are four things involved in controlling: First, **the establishment of performance standards.** Do you know when this is to be done with a missionary, or with a lady who is taking over a Sunday School department in the church, or with the man who is taking a job in the office of the

Bible Society, or with the man who is coming into a strategic position in the hospital? When must it be done? His perforformance standard must be stated before he starts to work. Missionary societies need to do this with their candidates before they ever sign on the dotted line and the Home Board accepts them. Do you know what kind of men you will attract when you clearly state the objectives of the group and the responsibilities of each individual? You will attract the courageous, the goal-oriented, the self-effacing, the self-sacrificing, always! But the standards have to be determined ahead of time. If they are not, and you have to go back and pick up the pieces, then it is more difficult but it can be done. Even in an old organization where a man goes and comes as and when he desires, it can be done. One day a lady who has visited a number of mission fields, said to me, "Do you know the great tragedy on the mission field? The great tragedy is — there is no must! I must get up! I must have my devotions. I must study. I must finish this language exam. I must see these people. I must prepare for this conference.

Management controlling is concerned with having an agreement with the individual that these are the standards toward which we are aiming. These standards are not unilaterally determined and handed down to the individual. Mr. A., up at the top, does not come along to a worker and say, "Look, you are going to do such and such." How does he do it? Mr. A., either on the field or back in the homeland, comes along and says, "Now, listen, our goal is this. Here are your gifts. Here is your calling according to your testimony. What standards of performance do you feel we should aim at together in order to accomplish this?" The man will always be harder on himself than you would be on him, if you were left to yourself to devise the standard unilaterally.

Then put it in writing. It is amazing how illiterate we become when it comes to management! We will not write things down! My first question to people with managerial problems is, "Does this fellow know his problem?" My second question is, "Is it written down and does he have a copy and do you have a copy? The answer ninety-nine times out of a hundred is "No." We must write down the standard of performance and give him a copy.

We who are in positions of leadership are required to love those under us supremely, but at the same time to hold them to the highest. The man at the top must constantly watch the performance of those under him. How many people should a man manage? There was a principle on this. A man should supervise as many people as he can effectively manage. What happens when he cannot manage all of the people? Someone else should manage a segment of them. The people we elect to managerial positions are already so busy that they cannot possibly oversee and scrutinize activities and procedures of others. But this is what is so absolutely essential.

The second thing is **performance measuring.** The man at the top must have some yardstick for measuring these activities. What kind of measurements do we need? We need to know when a fellow gets up and when he goes to bed. We need to know how many days he takes off each week and how many days he takes to go on vacation. We need to know when he is going on furlough and when he is coming back. I have been in missions all of these years and I still do not understand how this missionary is permitted to just unilaterally determine, "I'm going home and I'm coming back. I'll let you know when." What kind of measuring is this?

Performance measuring is based upon what we are doing and the goal we are collectively seeking to achieve. There is the standard of performance toward which we are all going to aim and there is the man who is going to measure the performance. This man agrees, "I want my performance measured."

Psychology tells us that one of the basic drives of the human being is his desire to achieve. There is a fire burning in the breast of every man to achieve something before he dies. This is especially true of every man in your mission or he would not be a missionary. He would be back home earning money and storing it away and living comfortably. He is a missionary because he wants to achieve something. If he seems to fight against management, he is not fighting because he is afraid that the superintendent or director is going to help him achieve something. He is fighting because he is afraid that this person is going to keep him from achieving something. He is so individualistic that he does not want the missionary society to hinder him from accomplishing something for the Lord and His kingdom. Management is not there to obstruct. While we push decisions down the ladder, what do we push up? Concern, help, direction. The man at the top should be able to say, "Look, the whole purpose of our being banded together, having bosses and subordinates and job descriptions and organizational charts and decisions made, our whole purpose is to facilitate the accomplishment of the thing that God has laid on your heart."

Thirdly, **performance evaluating** which is a little different from performance measuring. I do not know if I am reflecting Louis Allen's thought exactly, but I am trying to adapt it right now to our situation. To my way of thinking, in performance measuring we are concerned about **one** man. In performance evaluating we are concerned about appraising the relative value of this man's activities in relation to the activities of other men. This becomes even more difficult than performance measuring because with performance measuring we are concerned with one individual;

but with performance evaluating we are concerned with multi-individual situations.

In **performance correcting** we are concerned
with coaching, with providing the "how" to people
and, where necessary, stepping in and correcting
the situation that may have gone astray, always
with the objective in view. This is always the
goal toward which we are moving. A manager
should not correct simply to satisfy his own desires or wishes. This is why goal-orientation is
a necessity.

THE MANAGEMENT GRID

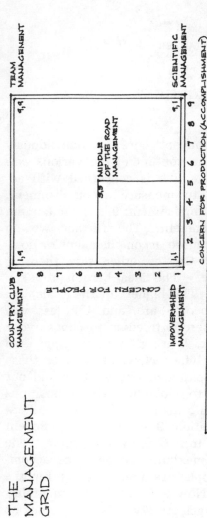

CONCERN FOR PEOPLE

9 — COUNTRY CLUB MANAGEMENT (1,9) ... TEAM MANAGEMENT (9,9)
8
7
6
5 — MIDDLE OF THE ROAD MANAGEMENT (5,5)
4
3
2
1 — IMPOVERISHED MANAGEMENT (1,1) ... SCIENTIFIC MANAGEMENT (9,1)

1 2 3 4 5 6 7 8 9

CONCERN FOR PRODUCTION (ACCOMPLISHMENT)

ISSUES	9,1	1,9	1,1	5,5	9,9
1. CREATIVITY	STIMULATING IN AN ANTI-ORGANIZATION WAY	STIFLES	NIL	LOW EXCEPT FOR PERSONAL SURVIVAL	HIGH-STIMULATING
2. COMMITMENT	HIGH, BUT IN ANTI-WAYS-UNIONS	HIGH PRO-ORGANIZATION	SURVIVE RATHER THAN CONTRIBUTE	HIGH	HIGH - A VOICE A STAKE COMMITMENT
3. CONFLICT	SUPPRESSION	SMOTHERING AVOID-KEEP LOW	NEUTRALITY	SPLITTING COMPROMISE	HIGH-CONFRONTED HEAD ON

CHAPTER XIII

MANAGEMENT GRID

I think the concept here is tremendously helpful in seeing the conflict of the various emphases. The bottom line is concerned with accomplishment, i.e. to measure accomplishment. 1 is the lowest accomplishment; 9 is the maximum or peak accomplishment. The further we go down this line, the more accomplishment or goal-oriented we are. On the other side there is concern for people. The idea here is to keep everybody happy. The higher up the scale you go, the happier people are, and the less you pressure them. There is freedom to choose your own type of work, bearing in mind your own happiness all the time. Now, of course, these things are in opposition to one another and our whole concern is to plot the various positions that are possible in a managerial situation. First you have a 9, 1 position: 9 on the accomplishment graph; 1 referring to a concern for people. The 9, 1 position has maximum concern for accomplishment but people are merely tools for the accomplishment. Now a 9, 1 attitude-mentality emphasis, or management style, is a laborious or toilsome type of management. This is where people are nothing more than necessary instruments or machines to accomplish tasks. This sort of management style exists in religious situations. Generally it is the product of the strong natural leader, though not always. It may be the product of a highly insecure but domineering type of individual who is not just a strong natural leader. The 9, 1 is what used to be called the scientific management approach. Maximum concern for accomplishment but a regard for people that is sub-human.

The other extreme is 1, 9 position, which says that the thing we are concerned about most is the happiness of these people. Whether we do anything or not is quite irrelevant. This we call a "country-club" type of management. This is where everyone works together around a swimming pool with tall cold drinks right at their elbow. Everybody is just happy, and at any gathering, or any situation, the whole concern is for happiness. This was epitomized in President Lyndon Johnson's speech one time when he turned to a heckler and said, "Why don't you people be happy?" — as though happiness were all that counts. The 1, 9 management style, then, is a "country-club" type of management.

Now unfortunately there is another style — namely 1, 1. This is impoverished management, where a man is neither motivated by a very great respect for the dignity of human personalities under his supervision, nor is he very much concerned about getting the product out the back door and on the train and shipped. Do not make the mistake of assuming that this kind of management style does not exist in Christian circles. It really does.

Another style of management comes up with a 5, 5 management style. This is a compromise type of management. It is neither dynamic nor is it dormant. It is active; it is alive, but not in such a way that you could tell it. It is a middle-of-the-road kind of management. The idea is that we want you to be happy, but not too happy. We will do anything to make you happy if it does not mean too much trouble. We want to achieve something; we really want to evangelize this country; but we are not going to sweat or toil about it. We are not going to get excited about it or "hot under the collar." That is sad! In a survey that has been done by UCLA, it was discovered from the estimation of thousands of managers in top-middle-lower echelons in America that 65% of industrial managers adjust their management style to this position. I reckon that if 65% of the people adjust to this position in industrial situations, probably 95% do it in religious situations. This is a tragic state of affairs.

There are other alternatives, but one thing that often happens is the wide-arc pendulum-swing where a fellow swings back and forth from 1, 9 to 9, 1. Someone shakes his complacency. He hears an inspirational sermon somewhere and he takes up a 9, 1 position. He decides to make sudden changes and clamps down on everybody. The result is that everybody becomes tense. Then someone comes along and says to him, "If you don't be good, we will not re-elect you." So, swinging back over to a 1, 9 country-club position, he apologizes and seeks to smooth out the situation. That is the wide-arc pendulum-swing. This is what you would wind up calling "statistical 5,5." It is not pure 5,5 or 9,1 or 1,9. It is just a swing between one and the other. A statistical 5,5 is more impoverished than 1,1 because no one ever knows where they stand. One day they are hard-hit and the next day affection is lavished upon them. It is characterized by inconsistency.

There is another position which is 9,9. This is a combination of concern for people in its maximum manifestation with a concern for production or accomplishment to its absolute maximum. This is the management style epitomized in the Lord Jesus Christ. He demonstrated the perfect combination of concern for people with concern for accomplishment.

There are three basic issues in any management style situation: creativity, commitment and conflict. These ingredients must be present in any wholesomely managed situation. What do these various management styles do to the various issues?

Creativity. What does 9,1 do to it? Remember 9,1 is a laborious, toilsome type of management.

Every effort is made to accomplish and produce without showing any concern for the workers. This is a very stimulating environment for creativity. However, it stimulates creativity in an anti-organizational way. This provokes people to figure out ways to beat the system. It is tremendously provocative in creativity, but provocative in the wrong direction! We create this situation in missions.

Commitment. 9, 1 creates high commitment, but always in anti-organizational ways. Usually people within the group form themselves around an insurrectionist who says, "Who cares for this society? Look how they are treating us! Let us join together and fight them." This is high in commitment, but in an anti-organizational way.

Conflict. What does 9,1 do to conflict? Conflict is a necessary ingredient in inter-personal human relationships. Are you aware of this? It was Lord Cromwell who said to one of his aides, "For heaven's sake, man, say 'no', so I'll know there are two of us!" There must be wholesome conflict. But 9,1 merely suppresses conflict. A worker has a complaint, but he is sternly rebuked and told to keep quiet.

What does 1,9 do to this issue? 1,9 is the concern for happiness. As to **creativity,** it stifles it. You have no creativity in country-club management because everyone wants things "as is" and they are not willing to do any forward thinking. As to **commitment,** it creates very high commitment, but in pro-organizational ways. This creates the centric group because it is oblivious to the goal. The 1,9 is never occupied with the worthwhile goal. Its goal is every man's happiness. As to **conflict,** it smothers it. Everything is all right. Do not disturb the situation.

What does 1,1 do? 1,1 is impoverished management. **Creativity** is nil. You do not have any creativity, any imagination, any forward thinking. As to **commitment,** the only commitment that you have in the 1,1 position is the commitment of survival. You are only committed insofar as it is necessary to keep your donors from dropping you and to keep your mission from sending you home. As to **conflict,** this produces absolute neutrality where everyone just shifts into neutral. There is no differing of opinions. There is no peppering interaction that produces creativity and dynamics. Everyone exists like a bunch of corpses thrown in side by side.

5,5 is the compromise position and this characterizes most religious organizations. What does it do to creativity? **Creativity** is very low in a 5,5 management style, except for personal survival. It does exist, not with respect to the work but with respect to personal survival. It is my work; these are my donors; this is my calling; this is my radio — 5,5! As to **commitment,** it tends to be high, simply because in the 5,5 position a man has to be committed in order to survive. He is neither secure in what he is accomplishing, nor in his relationship with other people. So instead, he finds his security in a very high level of commitment to a highly personal task, i.e. "God led me to this place," etc. What does this do to conflict? Whenever there is **conflict** there is splintering and there is compromise. There is neither substantial goal-orientation to insure the conflict being creative and wholesome, nor is there sufficient adjustment for keeping everyone happy. So this fellow gives a little, and somebody else gives a little, and the manager gives here and gives there, etc.

What about "team" management or the 9,9 position? **Creativity** is high and stimulating. Not only because a person knows that his boss recognizes value in his dignity, but because he knows that the whole organization with which he is associated is out to accomplish the goal that he has personally espoused. So creativity is high and stimulating. **Commitment** is very high because, as an individual, he has a stake and a voice and he is personally involved. It is interesting that effective management does not reduce this but maximizes it. Regarding **conflict,** it is high with interaction and a sharp exchange of ideas, because issues are confronted head-on. They are not suppressed. There must be high conflict, not personal hatred nor personal animosity, but personal inter-action that is stimulating and dynamic. Otherwise, one person with a group of puppets or figures could do as much as a whole group is doing. Conflict is where persons are pushed to be individuals on their own. Someone has well said, "Conformity in behaviour in an organization is essential, conformity in ideas in an organization is tragic." Hyper-democratic management will never know a 9,9 position. It will generally take the 5,5 position because there is such tension between the thought of re-election on the one hand and the question of how much can be accomplished on the other hand. Conflict does not necessarily mean fighting; perhaps "creative tension" would better describe it. Interaction, the idea of each person acting on the other, brings us up to our best. Generally we suppress interaction because the man at the top is afraid it is going to reflect on some of his deficiencies.

How do you educate your group? If a man suggests an idea and it is rejected, do you reject him also? If so, then this feeling is perpetuated and spreads like a fever among the group. On the other hand, is the group aware that a man's ideas will be tested, evaluated, dissected, and may be even thrown out, but that he himself will not suffer? Such an attitude shows maturity and creates a healthy atmosphere. Our problem is basically a management problem in the sense described in the PLOC outline. If there is conflict in the sense of fighting, then the man steps in. Why? Because we are not accomplishing our goal when we are fighting. Are you fighting simply to perpetuate an organization? Surely not.

But let us have conflict that will enable us to accomplish our objectives as a group.

Conformity of behaviour is essential, but conformity in ideas is tragic. When we conform in our ideas, and everybody has to think the same ideas, then we stagnate. Most missionary societies are in a state of stagnation today. From time to time the sharing of our ideas on various aspects of our work, such as finance and furloughs, produces a healthy situation. We need to encourage and stimulate our co-workers to express themselves. However, we do not implement everything that occurs to us. We must have a system of evaluation, scrutinizing, appraising and testing before we implement. I talked to a candidate sometime ago who had been turned down by a certain mission. I may be wrong, but my estimate of the situation was that they turned him down because he was too creative. I do not think he will go to the mission field now. That is tragic!

Let us picture in our mind a missionary organization of three hundred people represented by twenty-five charts. When new workers come in, usually they are placed in the lower echelon of the chart. They have a specific function and assignment, and, incidentally, it should be made clear to the new workers that even though they are low on the chart they are not inferior socially. Each position is vital to the function and goal of the organization; but unfortunately, most people think only of status.

A new worker is accepted by the missionary organization. What do we do in the mission? In a lot of missions they say, "So you are joining our group. For a year, or two years, you will not have any vote; for a term you will be a junior missionary and will not have any say. Now, do not open your mouth." Is this right? Is there a better way? Do we need a screening process where the mentality and the goal and the function of the group is adequately represented to this fellow so that when he comes in he is a part of the organization? Why do we stifle? It is because we are afraid, we are insecure, we are not sure where we stand and where we are going and how to do it, etc. The moment new people come into our mission, or into our church, we are changing our mission and our church. The addition of one personality to our church alters that church. We have to screen so that we do not get people in who are undesirable, but let us determine what is undesirable. Is it the creativity that is undesirable?

Chapter XIV

CONCLUSION

Eighty-five to ninety percent of the participants in management seminars never do anything about it. The purpose of this book is to INTRODUCE the subject of management to Christian workers. Do not assume that you know everything about management because you have read this book! If this is all you have ever studied or read on the subject of management, then you know very little. To give anyone the impression (or to be under the impression yourself) that you are a knowledgeable person in the field of management will only lead to trouble. This book is an introduction to the subject. What you do after this is of real significance. Hundreds and hundreds of people have come to management seminars that I have taught. However, we find that only 10% to 15% of those who attend ever do anything about what they learn. Many people go away and talk about it; they have been impressed, and some are even excited about the relevance of much of this material. But that is not enough! A little knowledge is a very dangerous thing, particularly when it comes to management. This sort of thing takes work, work, work! You have to experiment. You have to revise it.

You have to adapt it. You have to discuss it. It is worthwhile if you persevere.

Another point is, do not assume that this is a substitute for something else. It is not a substitute for prayer, nor for the fulness of the Holy Spirit. Management offers tools that can help you if you implement them and use them. But the very best tools are useless unless we wield them and use them.

Do not start wagging your tongue, showing people how much you know. You will alienate them. They will resent your possessing knowledge that they do not have, and you might even get your neck in a good tight noose if you are not very careful. Do something before you do a lot of talking. Start with yourself — with your job description, your own objectives, your own organizational chart. Start with an effort to appraise your own communication. Start with yourself. You will keep this best by example, not by word, and if you apply words too soon, you are going to be in real trouble.

Many management teachers have emphasized that if you are ever to do anything with management, you will begin it within two weeks after this course ends. What you do not begin within two weeks, you will probably not do anything about. It will go on the shelf and collect dust. Three months from now you will go right back to the tyranny of the urgent at the expense of the important. It happens to hundreds and hundreds of people, not just in Christian work, but in industry too, all the time. Young executives go away to a seminar. They come back and their desks are piled high. Immediately they feel that they must deal with everything that is on their desks. These are the urgent matters lying at hand. Management is important, but the pressures of the urgent push all they received at the seminar away into the background. They subject themselves to the urgent at the expense of the important. What you are ever going to do in management, you will probably begin in the next two weeks.

Write a report on the helpful information you have received relative to your own work and your own situation. Start with yourself and your own work. A written report will put in solid memorable form what you have received, and it is a good way to relate the information, or relay the information from the shelf to other people.

Having worked out an organizational chart, do not expect to push the ideas you have learned and believe to be useful up your chart. It will not work. Begin where you are. Educate in other directions first, i.e., down and sideways. There may even be the desire to change the constitution of your organization. Don't! Start applying the management principles in the organization as it is.

To summarize, here is WHAT NOT TO DO:

1. Do not assume that you know everything about management.

2. Do not assume that management is a substitute for prayer or the fulness of the Holy Spirit.

3. Do not go to the organization and tell them how much they need to adopt these principles.

4. Do not expect to push these ideas up your organizational chart.

5. Do not try to change the constitution of your organization.

Here is WHAT TO DO:

1. Start within two weeks after reading this book, and start with yourself.

2. Write a report to your boss.

3. Begin to educate in four directions, i.e. down, sideways, and finally up.

4. Set aside some time to study management further.

5. Start a file of management information.